This book belongs to

Creole Made Easy

with the
Creole Sausage Queen

Creole Made Easy

with the
Creole Sausage Queen

Written by Julie Frederick Vaucresson
Foreword by Poppy Tooker

PELICAN PUBLISHING
NEW ORLEANS

The word "Pelican" and the depiction of a pelican are trademarks of Arcadia Publishing Company Inc. and are registered in the U.S. Patent and Trademark Office.

ISBN 9781455627981

Food photography courtesy of Shawn Colin
All other photography courtesy of Vaucresson family collection

Printed in China
Published by Pelican Publishing
New Orleans, LA
www.pelicanpub.com

In gratitude to my family, my love for you is what motivates me; without each of you, this book wouldn't have been possible

My Family—VJ, Julie, Vance, and Hilary

Contents

Sonny at the Fest by Connie Kittock

The Great Mystery of Creole

What does it mean to be Creole and who or what may be called Creole today? Creole tomatoes, shrimp Creole, and Creole cream cheese are part of our local vernacular with "Creole" regularly proclaimed on fine dining menus with pride. Julie Frederick Vaucresson and her husband Vance, along with generations of their ancestors, have always proudly identified as Creole New Orleanians.

Prior to Hurricane Katrina, my contact with the Vaucresson family was largely limited to their New Orleans Jazz and Heritage Festival booth where I enjoyed many a hot sausage po' boy over the years. Then in November 2006, *GQ* magazine published a piece by writer Alan Richman questioning the entire concept of Creole people and their food. Displaying an abundance of cultural ignorance, Mr. Richman stated, "Supposedly, Creoles can be found in and around New Orleans. I have never met one and suspect they are a faerie folk, like leprechauns, rather than an indigenous race. The myth is that once, long ago, Creoles existed."

Richman's outrageous words incited a call to action that resulted in a meeting orchestrated by longtime friend and collaborator, Lolis Eric Elie. Over calas and Creole cream cheese, Vance Vaucresson and I joined forces with Lolis to defend our mutual heritage and the city we all love. That was the day we met *New York Times* writer Kim Severson who was tasked with deciphering the supposed mystery. After doing much investigative reporting, Severson's efforts resulted in a *New York Times* article entitled, "'Fairie Folk' Strike Back With Fritters."

That day, Vance and I forged a friendship which has strengthened through years as I came to know his wife Julie and their children, Hilary and VJ. It has been an honor and a privilege to watch the indomitable Vaucressons fight their way back through seemingly insurmountable odds to the historic corner of St. Bernard and Roman in the Seventh Ward.

When Julie Vaucresson asked me to collaborate with her on this book, I immediately agreed, recognizing the opportunity to play a part in illustrating Creole culture fully, in a way never done before. After many long discussions on the volatile subject, Vance Vaucresson's message is clear. In his words, "If you were born here, no matter what your race or ethnicity may be, you *are* Creole in the truest sense of the word. Creole has unfortunately become misunderstood and racialized. Whether you used the French word, *créole,* or the Spanish, *criollo,* the word designated you as native."

No matter if your family came from France, Spain, West Africa, or in later times, Haiti, your offspring were known as Creole. Vance's great unifying umbrella includes later settlers as well. "The children of the Sicilians, the Irish, and more recently the Vietnamese—they are truly Creole too. All the wonderful ethnicities who came here and settled, once their children were born, they became part of a unified culture. If we acknowledge our common cultural heritage, we could be the forebearers of bringing our community together," Vance reflected.

How has Creole become so terribly misunderstood? Vance traces the issue back to the original Americans who came to New Orleans following the Louisiana Purchase. "Those British and Americans were trying to understand who was what. There existed a caste system where French Afro-Creoles were often by-products of White landowners owing to the "*plaçage*" tradition here. White landowners took Black mistresses, and their children were born free people of color. Many were educated in France, gifted land, and even owned slaves themselves," Vance said. "But whether White or of mixed race, French was their primary language and they all identified as Creole," which thoroughly confused the English speakers.

After Reconstruction, "colorism kicked in," Vance said. Two thirds of people who were Creole no longer wanted to be associated with that term. By the early twentieth century, the "one drop rule" became a legal race classification, indicating anyone with one Black ancestor must be considered non-white and subject to segregation laws of the day.

This resulted in prejudice even among Afro-Creoles, where darker skinned people were often ostracized within their own community. The rigid restrictions and marginalized experience led many to "*passé blanc,*" Vance recounted. "Many light skinned folks left and went to California. There, the "c" on their birth certificates that indicated "colored" at home in Louisiana, meant Caucasian in California. In my own family, we had a relative who lived as White in California and raised a family there. Several years ago, their grandchildren contacted us after researching their ancestry. It was quite a shock to them to learn that their New Orleans family identifies as African American.

"The New Orleans Seventh Ward is the mecca of our Creole culture. It is a bedrock of cultural, familial history." Vance urged, "So many people feel lost. They don't understand they are Creole and need to connect to the culture. For these absent Creoles to understand and appreciate their place, they must come back, set their feet on the ground, smell the air, and look around at all the landmarks still standing. Speak with your neighbors . . . your family. Find that connection, that root of who you are and the cultural significance of your place in its history."

Between the pages of this book, you will discover the nuanced flavors that represent more than three hundred years of Creole cooking. Don't be surprised if before too long, you begin to identify as Creole yourself. The Vaucressons welcome us all into the rich layers of the Creole community, a place we can always find common ground through culture and learn we are all truly more alike than you realize.

Poppy Tooker

My Frederick family talking
Creole; Momma, Joey, Angela,
Julie, and Rivers

Vaucresson Booth at New
Orleans Jazz and Heritage
Festival

Creole Talk

Listen closely on any Seventh Ward street corner and you might catch some talk in a native tongue unlike any other. Creole patois has strong French roots often difficult to clearly trace back to the original language. The conversation that wafts through screened back doors is as spicy and mysterious as the food. Even the back door itself plays a role. What's known as "door poppin'," is basic, neighborhood reconnaissance. "The screen door might be closed but you could put your nose up against it to see just what your neighbors are up to," Vance explained.

A conversation may begin with "Come I tell you," often where the "caunting" begins. "She over there caunting," Vance said laughingly as an example. "Caunt," the Creole word for "gossip" is often compounded with "movasant" when things get messy. One neighbor might tell another, "I heard she messin' with that man around the corner," only to receive the admonishment, "Oh, you betta stop with all that movasant!"

"In years past when Monday was wash day, you'd see neighbors caunting over the fence," Vance remembered. "I was working on song lyrics with New Orleans musician Paul Sanchez and my cousin John Boutté. I sang to them, 'My mamére Ti na with her movasant making ma chou caunt over fresh ton ton.' The lyrics worked, but Sanchez demanded to know, "What the hell does that mean?" Vance explained it meant a close female relative was talking some messy gossip while enjoying her "ton ton," the Creole name for the rounded end of fresh, New Orleans French bread, well buttered and often enjoyed with café au lait.

Family ties are everything in the close-knit Creole community. When seeing a new baby for the first time it was often said, "They done been here before," or "That's the spirit of my grandmother in that chile."

Those terms evoke such emotions generationally. "Hey bébé," "chére bébé," or even just "ma baby," these are all terms of endearment showered on hungry Jazz Fest folks. "It's actually part of our training when people come to work the booth with us. We expect you to use at least one term of endearment for every few customers," Julie said with a smile.

No wonder so many festival goers start their day with an extra serving of Creole style love, a Vaucresson family tradition.

Creole Made Easy

Easy

with the
Creole Sausage Queen

Julie Wauuuresson

Frederick family growing up—Angela, Joey, Rivers, Julie, and Momma

CHAPTER ONE

To Begin

The radio was playing Maze's "Golden Time of Day." As I approached the screen door, I could hear my mother humming along with the music. The windows and back door were open, letting fresh air in and the smell of good food out. I could hear the sizzle of the hot sausage and grease popping as I approached the kitchen door. Recognizing that spicy pork sausage scent frying in a pan, I spotted two loaves of French bread on the table. They were cut open, slathered with mayo, and layered with lettuce and tomatoes. Bags of Lays plain potato chips and two liters of Barq's root beer were on the table as well. Ironically, dinner that evening was a family favorite, hot sausage po' boys with root beer . . . it didn't get much better.

I joined my siblings sitting around the kitchen table, my older sister, Angela, big brother, Rivers, and the baby of the family, Joey, and we ate our po' boys and chips, drank root beer, and laughed and joked with each other. As usual, we were having fun. Anyone looking in would have sworn it was a special occasion, but this was just a regular dinner for us. There really wasn't anything special about my household growing up. This could be a scene from many homes throughout the city of New Orleans.

My mom, Josette Broussard Frederick was widowed with four kids at the young age of thirty-nine. She worked, took care of us, and made sure we had whatever we needed—especially dinner. I never understood what it took to make everything happen. I still don't know how she did it, but she made it look so easy.

Chicken with a Short Gravy

Yields 6 servings

My sister Angela has lived away from New Orleans for over twenty years. Whenever she comes home, Mom always cooks her favorite meal, chicken with rice and gravy and corn. Mom calls this a "short gravy," which basically means pot drippings with no flour or roux added. While the chicken is browning, bits stick to the bottom of the pan. When stock or water is added, those bits are scraped up from the pan's bottom, deglazing it for a "short gravy."

3 lbs. frying chicken, cut into pieces, skin on
Creole seasoning to taste
Black pepper to taste
1 tbsp. granulated garlic
1 tbsp. granulated onion
½ medium onion, chopped
1 bunch green onions, chopped
½ medium bell pepper, chopped
½ tsp. garlic, chopped
½ cup chicken broth

Season chicken with Creole seasoning, black pepper, granulated garlic and onion, and brown chicken on all sides in a heavy pot, then set aside. In the same pot, sauté onion, green onions, bell pepper, and garlic for 3 minutes.

Return chicken to the pot and add the chicken broth. Deglaze the pot by stirring, thoroughly scraping all the browned bits from the bottom of the pot to deglaze.

Cover and reduce heat to a low fire and simmer for 30 minutes. Serve with cooked rice and corn to have it like Angela.

Easter Sunday growing up — Rivers, Julie, Momma, and Joey

Pork and Rice

Yields 6 servings

When we were growing up, we would ask Mom to cook "New Iberia food." These were special one-pot meals she learned to love growing up there. Things like okra, fresh corn, chicken and sausage gumbo, and pork and rice were all "New Iberia" food to us. Pork and rice is still one of my younger brother Joey's favorite meals.

1 lb. pork steak cut into one-inch cubes
Creole seasoning to taste
Black pepper to taste
1 tsp. granulated garlic
1 tbsp. vegetable oil
1 medium onion, chopped
1 medium bell pepper, chopped
1 stalk celery, chopped
½ cup chicken broth
3 cloves garlic, chopped
1 cup long grain rice, cooked

Season meat with Creole seasoning, black pepper, and granulated garlic.

Heat oil in a heavy 3-quart skillet. Brown pork on all sides, then add onions, bell pepper, and celery. Sauté together for 5 minutes. Add chicken broth and garlic.

Cover and simmer for 5 minutes. Stir in cooked rice, remove from heat, and serve.

Momma and her sister, Claudette Sonnier, in New Iberia, Louisiana

Rice Dressing

Yields 12 servings

My mother is from New Iberia, Louisiana. We spent lots of time there when we were young, and after Hurricane Katrina, we lived there for two years. I have fond memories of the smell of sugar cane burning, the persimmon tree, my grandfather's smoke house, and zydeco music. The food was delicious with rich gravies, chicken and sausage gumbo, brown jambalaya, and rice dressing. My mother didn't make rice dressing, but her sister Claudette did. It was one of my favorites. We always loved visiting Aunt Claudette and having her rice dressing at dinner. When I started making it, I added our hot sausage to it for an extra kick and burst of flavor.

3 tbsp. vegetable oil
1 lb. Vaucresson's Creole Hot Sausage, out of the casing
1 lb. ground sirloin
1 lb. liver and gizzards, boiled and ground
Creole seasoning to taste
Cayenne pepper to taste
1 large onion, chopped
1 medium bell pepper, chopped
2 stalks celery, chopped
3 cloves garlic, chopped
1 cup water
1 dash Kitchen Bouquet
1¼ cups green onions, chopped
3 cups long grain rice, cooked
3 green onions, thinly sliced

Heat oil in a skillet. Brown hot sausage, ground sirloin, liver and gizzards, and season with Creole seasoning and cayenne pepper. Stir in onions, bell pepper, celery, and garlic and cook until wilted. Add the water, Kitchen Bouquet, and 1 cup of the chopped green onions. Reduce heat and cook for 45 minutes, stirring occasionally.

In a large mixing bowl, combine the meat mixture with the rice, being careful not to overmix, which can cause the rice to get mushy. Serve with the remaining green onions sprinkled on top.

Crawfish Cornbread

Yields 8 servings

New Iberia holds a special place in my heart. I spent many summers there with my many cousins. I even gave birth to my daughter, Hilary there after Hurricane Katrina. When we're in New Iberia there is always lots of family, laughter, and the most delicious foods. Crawfish cornbread was a casserole that my absolute favorite uncle, Parran Gene would cook. This casserole is one of Vance's favorites too.

2 boxes Jiffy cornbread
¼ cup butter
1 medium yellow onion, chopped
¼ red bell pepper, chopped
¼ green bell pepper, chopped
3-4 cloves of garlic, finely chopped
1 jalepeño, seeded and chopped (optional)
1 8-oz. can tomato sauce
1 15.25-oz. can whole kernel corn
1 15.25-oz. can cream style corn
Creole Seasoning to taste
Black pepper to taste
1 tsp. onion powder
1 tsp. garlic powder
1 lb. Louisiana crawfish tails
¼ cup parsley, chopped
2 cups shredded cheddar cheese

Preheat oven to 350 degrees. Prepare cornbread according to the package and put in a greased casserole pan and set aside.

Melt butter in a pan, add onions and bell peppers, and sauté until soft. Add garlic and jalepeño and sauté an additional 3-5 minutes. Add tomato sauce and corn and simmer together for 3-5 minutes. Then add Creole seasoning, black pepper, and onion and garlic powders.

Add the crawfish and cook for about 5 minutes. Remove from heat and stir in parsley. Spoon the crawfish and corn mixture on top of the uncooked cornbread and top with cheese.

Bake covered at 350 degrees until the cornbread is baked through. Cut into squares and serve warm.

White Bread

Yields 3 loaves

When we were children, there were days when we would come home from school and smell mom's fresh, baked bread as soon as we hit the front door. We would sit at the kitchen table and have a hot slice with melted butter. I always enjoyed watching the bread making process. My mother would have the dough in a big mixing bowl covered with a dish towel. Often, she would put the bowl in the oven to let it rise. She said the pilot light made it warm in there, even though it wasn't on. I loved to watch her punch it down and see it deflate. It was a long process, but oh so worth it.

3 cups milk, heated
2 packages yeast
¼ cup shortening, melted
1 tbsp. salt
¼ cup sugar
2 eggs, beaten
9-10 cups sifted flour

Set aside 1 cup milk to cool. When lukewarm, add yeast and stir until dissolved. Allow it to proof for 5 minutes. When it's bubbling, you know the yeast is active. To the remaining hot milk, add shortening, salt, and sugar. Allow to cool to lukewarm.

In a mixing bowl, combine proofed yeast with milk mixture and add the eggs. Gradually add enough flour to make a soft dough and beat thoroughly.

Turn out on a lightly floured board and knead until dough becomes elastic and doesn't stick to the board. Place in a bowl greased with shortening. Cover and let rise in a warm place until doubled in bulk, about 1 hour.

After it has doubled in bulk, punch dough down. Divide dough and shape into 3 loaves. Place in 3 greased, 9x5x3-inch loaf pans. Cover and let rise again in a warm place until the center is slightly higher than the edges of the pan, about 1 hour.

Bake at 400 degrees for about 50 minutes until the crust is browned. Serve with lots of butter.

Coconut Shortbread Cookies

Yields 16 cookies

Coconut has always been a favorite of mine. For Easter, I would get miniature Mounds candy. For my birthday, I would have German chocolate cake. When my mother made coconut shortbread cookies, I would try to hide them so I could have them all. These cookies are simple goodness, just like mom.

1 cup butter, softened
¾ cup sugar
1 tsp. vanilla extract
⅛ tsp. salt
1¾ cups flour
1 cup flaked coconut

Cream butter and sugar together until smooth. Mix in vanilla extract. Slowly add the salt, flour, and coconut, mixing well with each addition. Roll dough into a loaf, wrap in plastic and chill overnight.

Slice dough into 1-inch slices and place on a parchment lined baking sheet. Bake at 325 degrees for 20-25 minutes until lightly browned. Store in a tin to keep fresh.

Rivers Frederick, M.D.

Eloise Clarke Frederick

CHAPTER TWO

The Fredericks, Home in the Seventh Ward

Both the Vaucressons and the Fredericks have long lived in what might be New Orleans' most Creole neighborhood, the Seventh Ward. Populated by free people of color before the Civil War, it was a gracious neighborhood lined with shady old oaks. The St. Bernard Market (which later became Circle Market) was located there. That was where Vaucresson had his original butcher's stall and where my father-in-law Sonny, opened his sausage business. It's also the place my father was raised.

My grandfather died before I was born, but the larger-than-life story of Dr. Rivers Frederick lived on. Born in 1874 to a sharecropper on Drouillard Plantation in Pointe Coupee, handsome, fair skinned Rivers left home at twenty-six for college in New Orleans. He graduated from Straight College (later to be Dillard University) and enrolled in medical school. When Rivers realized New Orleans' segregated hospitals would not allow Black residents to train, he completed his education in the Midwest and was the first African American to graduate from Chicago College of Physicians and Surgeons. He returned home to Point Coupee, becoming the town's doctor and treating patients both Black and White.

His marriage to a White woman ignited racial tensions in the small town, and the couple eventually settled in New Orleans where for decades he served as chief of surgery at Flint-Goodrich Hospital. He and his wife Adele raised two daughters, Pearl and Lolita in a gracious home on Upperline Street.

With his sharp intellect and keen business sense, Rivers created many prosperous endeavors within New Orleans' Black community. He was a founder of the Louisiana Life Insurance Company and served as board president for many years. Rivers was instrumental in growing the company into the largest Black-owned insurance agency in the South. He later opened the Louisiana Undertaking Company, another Seventh Ward landmark.

My beautiful grandmother,
Eloise Clarke Frederick

My grandfather, Dr. Rivers Frederick on
the steps of Flint Goodrich Hospital

My parents, Rivers
Frederick II and
Josette Broussard,
at their wedding

When his first wife Adele passed away at the age of sixty-five, Rivers married my grandmother, Eloise Clarke. At twenty-four, Eloise was a beautiful, blue-eyed blonde whose parents both identified as Black and hailed from Belize. Their only child, my father, Rivers II was born in 1939.

My grandfather was a very generous man who accumulated great wealth and used it to better his community. He founded the New Orleans chapter of the NAACP and helped fund the local chapter of the National Urban League. Rivers donated so generously to the Orleans Parish school system, a Seventh Ward school was named after him. At the time of his death, my grandfather was said to be worth 1.5 million dollars.

Like my paternal grandfather, my mom Josette Broussard was the child of a New Iberia sharecropper. She grew up steeped in Creole country tradition, eating the gravy laden dishes of South Louisiana. Momma skipped a grade to graduate early and came to New Orleans with her sister Claudette to attend Xavier University. The two girls lived with Jewish families, caring for the children and helping with the housework in exchange for room and board. My mom learned to cook Creole city food from the family's housekeeper and gained an appreciation for setting a fine table there. Mom's best friend introduced her to my dad, Rivers, on a blind date. Mom graduated at the age of twenty and married him the following year.

I didn't see much of my grandfather's opulent wealth growing up. My father was left with the funeral home. He wasn't a funeral director or undertaker, just the business manager as his father had been. With Mom running the flower shop, it really was a family affair.

As small children, the Louisiana Undertaking Company was our home away from home. Dad's funeral home driver would often bring us to school and pick us up afterwards in the company's long, black limousine. We were embarrassed for our friends to see us getting out of the limo, so we'd sneak around the back. I remember games of hide and seek in the funeral home's coffin display room along with afterschool treats and other meals in the home-like kitchen there.

My dad passed away too early. He was just thirty-nine when he died, leaving mom alone with us four kids. Struggling to make ends meet, mom sold the funeral business and went back to work as a second-grade schoolteacher, a job she held for decades.

Despite her troubles, we never wanted for a thing. Mom served a delicious family meal every night and Sunday dinner was always something special. Whatever we had, Mom always taught us to share.

Momma's Crab Pie

Yields 6 slices

During childhood, the things I loved most about Easter mornings were the tons of candy, dyed eggs, and crab pie. Mom would feed us her rich and delicious crab pie before going to mass. Our whole family looked forward to waking up to check our Easter baskets before eating a slice of momma's crab pie. When I make this for my family, one taste brings back all those happy Easter memories.

1 9-inch pie crust
4 tbsp. butter
1 medium to small onion, chopped
2-3 cloves garlic, finely chopped
1 tbsp. flour
½ cup mayonnaise
½ cup half and half
2 large eggs
Creole seasoning to taste
Black pepper to taste
1 tsp. garlic powder
2 cups shredded sharp cheddar cheese
1 16-oz. container of crabmeat (shells picked out)

Preheat oven to 350 degrees. Prick holes in the pie crust and bake for 5-8 minutes, then reserve.

Melt butter and sauté onions until soft. Add garlic and sauté an additional 3 minutes. Sprinkle flour over the onions and garlic and cook for 5 minutes, then set aside.

In a large bowl, whisk together mayonnaise, half and half, and eggs. Add Creole seasoning, black pepper, garlic powder, and cheddar cheese, mixing together well. Gently fold in crabmeat, being careful not to break apart the lumps. Pour crab mixture into the pie crust and bake at 350 degrees for 30-40 minutes until pie is firm and golden.

This can be baked in a casserole dish without having a crust.

New Orleans Red Beans and Rice

Yields 8 servings

You can find red beans served in homes and restaurants in New Orleans every Monday. Monday was washday and while women tended to their laundry, they would put a pot of beans on the stove and let them simmer all day. There are many different recipes for beans, with variations ranging from what seasoning meats to use, whether to soak the beans soak or not, and Crock-pot or stovetop cooking methods. But one thing most New Orleanians do agree on is Camellia Brand dried beans. They really do make a difference!

1 lb. pickled pork
1 large onion, chopped
½ green bell pepper, chopped
2 celery stalks, chopped
1 bay leaf
6 cups water or chicken stock
1 lb. Camellia dried red beans, soaked overnight
1 lb. smoked sausage, cut into 1-inch pieces
1 lb. Vaucresson's Creole Hot Sausage,
  fully cooked and cut into 1-inch pieces
2 smoked turkey wings, if available
¼ cup Italian parsley, chopped
1 tbsp. garlic powder
Creole seasoning to taste
Black pepper to taste
8 cups cooked rice

In a large saucepot, bring the pickled pork to a full boil. Boil for 10 minutes. Drain and rinse well. Set the pork aside.

In an 8-qt. stock pot, combine onion, bell pepper, celery, bay leaf, water or stock, dried beans, and pickled pork. Bring to a boil then reduce to a simmer. Cook for 2½-3 hours, stirring frequently to make the beans creamy. Add more water/chicken stock as needed.

Add sausages and smoked turkey wings (if available) then cook for another hour, stirring frequently until beans are soft and creamy. Add parsley and garlic powder. Finish with Creole seasoning, black pepper to taste. Serve over cooked rice.

Creole Shepherd's Pie

Yields 8 servings

There are certain meals from my childhood that we were always super excited about. Shepherd's pie was one of them. My siblings and I would aggravate my mother with a barrage of questions like, "Is it ready yet? How much longer?" What could be better than meat, potatoes, and cheese? I updated the recipe using our Creole hot sausage mixed with ground chuck for a spicy kick.

1 lb. Yukon gold potatoes
1 tsp. salt
1 lb. ground chuck
½ lb. Vaucresson's Creole Hot Sausage, out of the casing
8 tbsp. butter, with 1 tbsp. reserved
1 medium onion, chopped
½ green bell pepper, chopped
3 cloves garlic, finely chopped
1 8-oz. can tomato sauce
1 cup chicken broth
½ cup heavy whipping cream
2 cups shredded sharp cheddar cheese
1 tsp. garlic powder
Creole seasoning to taste
Black pepper to taste

Preheat oven to 350 degrees. Peel potatoes and cut into quarters. Boil in salted water until soft and easy to mash. Drain, peel, and reserve. Thoroughly mix ground chuck with sausage. Set aside.

In a heavy skillet, melt 1 tbsp. butter over medium heat. Add onion and bell pepper and sauté until soft. Add garlic and sauté garlic for 3 minutes. Add meat mixture to the skillet and brown together with seasoning vegetables. Drain off any excess grease. Add tomato sauce to the meat mixture and simmer together for 5 minutes.

In a saucepan, combine potatoes with the remaining 7 tbsp. of butter and chicken broth. Use a hand mixer to get the potatoes creamy, adding more liquid if necessary.

In a 9x13-inch casserole pan, alternate layers of meat and potatoes. Top with shredded cheese. Bake for approximately 20 minutes until the meat mixture bubbles beneath the potatoes.

*Can add corn and other veggies to the meat.

Popcorn Balls

Yields 8 balls

Growing up, Mardi Gras was truly something special. In those days, there were still neighborhood parades, and we were fortunate to have two of them pass right in front of our house. Every Carnival season, we would host an open house and invite friends, family, and anyone we knew to stop by. My mother always made popcorn balls and candy apples for the open house that everyone looked forward to. She would set up a table outside with the balls and apples as grab and go, and did they go! Now when I go to parades uptown, I always see men with carts selling their wares on the street before the parades. They always have popcorn balls and candy apples which always brings a smile to my face.

3 tbsp. vegetable oil
1½ cup popcorn kernels
1 cup Steen's Cane Syrup
1 cup white sugar
1 tsp. vanilla
⅓ tsp. salt

Heat oil on high in a large pot with a lid. Test to see if oil is ready by dropping a couple of popcorn kernels in. When the test kernels pop, the oil is ready. Add the remaining kernels and cover. As the kernels begin to pop, listen closely for the popping to slow down. Set popcorn aside to cool.

Heat cane syrup and sugar in a large pot to 350 degrees. Use a candy thermometer to test the temperature. Add vanilla and salt, stirring just enough to mix. Combine the syrup with the popcorn and mix well. Form the popcorn into balls and set on wax paper to cool.

Mardi Gras Day—Julie, Hilary, and VJ

Candy Apples

Yields 8 servings

Candy apples are a fun food. They can be tricky to make, but once you get them right, they are a special treat. I love that candy apples are associated with good times like parades, carnivals, and birthday parties. When mom made her candy apples, we all knew fun was just around the corner.

8 small to medium apples (I use Red Delicious)
¼ cup corn syrup
2 cups granulated sugar
¾ cup water
½ tsp. red food coloring

Wash apples well to remove any wax. Pull out the apple stems. Insert a stick into the apples where the stem was. Mix the corn syrup, sugar, and water in a saucepan. Boil until the mixture reaches the hard ball stage, about 300 degrees on a candy thermometer. Add a few drops of food coloring into the saucepan and stir until the candy is evenly colored. Dip each apple into the candy, allowing any excess to drip off, then place on a parchment paper lined baking sheet to cool.

Tip: Make sure the candy mixture reaches 300 degrees. If it isn't hard enough, it will be soft and sticky.

Vance's grandfather, Robert
Lovinsky Vaucresson

Robert Lovinsky Vaucresson
and Sonny, Vance's dad

CHAPTER THREE

The Vaucressons, Back in the Seventh Ward

Just like my family, the Vaucressons also have deep Seventh Ward roots. During his years operating the sausage business on the corner of St. Bernard and N. Roman, Vance's dad, Sonny Vaucresson was the heart of the neighborhood. While my family, the Fredericks, had owned an undertaking business, folks always joked that Sonny "buried more people than an undertaker," because if he could help, he would. Sonny bought sports uniforms, made donations, often anonymously, for school uniforms. He cashed checks, made loans—he was a friend to all.

The Vaucresson's New Orleans story begins in 1899, when Vance's great-grandfather, a French Polish Jew named Lovinsky Vaucresson arrived here with his wife, Odile Gaillard, a French Creole woman. Their son, Robert Lovinsky Vaucresson was a butcher who quickly gained a following with his delicious sausage. From a butcher's stall in the St. Bernard Market, his business grew into a multigenerational family enterprise; a meat market on the corner of North Johnson and St. Bernard in the Seventh Ward.

Robert married three times. He had three daughters with his first wife and no children with the second, but his third wife, Julia gave him a son, Robert "Sonny" Vaucresson. His older sisters Glenda and Marlene, doted on the beautiful, blonde-haired, blue-eyed boy. "He could do no wrong," they would say.

Although Sonny learned the butcher's trade from his father, he dreamed bigger than the meat market. After military service, he attended Xavier University, but when his father died before graduation, Sonny found himself running the family business. He enlisted his older brothers-in-law and expanded into the liquor trade. Sonny went on to operate a cigarette company while shrewdly investing in real estate.

When it came to good looks, Sonny found his match in Vance's beautiful mom, Geraldine Dave. Geraldine was the first Black woman to integrate the public library. Although New Orleans

Sonny Vaucresson

Vance's mom, Geraldine Dave Vaucresson

Public Libraries were legally integrated in 1951, the old, racially segregated ways died hard in some neighborhoods. Geraldine was employed as a librarian before marrying Sonny.

To make Blacks feel welcome at the Napoleon branch, light-complected Geraldine was hired. Although there were protestors outside of the library when she arrived, Geraldine sailed right through. She was successful because her looks confused people who were looking to harass the new Black librarian. At the same time, everyone in the Black community knew who Geraldine was and where she worked, so it helped them make that transition.

Sonny and his wife, Geraldine, had three sons, Robert, Rene, and my husband, Vance who all started working in the sausage business while they were still in grade school. When Vance was a senior at Morehouse College, his dad paid him a visit. "Son, you know I've got this business, and I really need some help. I really wish you'd come back and work in the family business," Sonny begged him. Vance had a job offer from Kraft General Foods, but he promised his dad he'd consider coming home.

Taking into consideration what a rare chance it was to be part of a multigenerational business in the Black community, Vance returned to New Orleans and went to work with his father. He'd learned all this business theory in college, but Sonny had years and years of actually running a business and handling the trials and tribulations involved. Vance always says, if he and Sonny didn't fuss every day at work, he'd think something was wrong, a family tradition he has continued with me!

In 1970, Sonny purchased a building on the corner of North Roman and St. Bernard Avenue intending to construct his own USDA processing facility. The racist Louisiana politicians of the time threw him every roadblock they could find, but after thirteen years of persistence, Sonny opened his facility in 1983. This transformed his business into a viable wholesale concern with the ability to sell to grocery chains and other large accounts.

Five years into working together, Vance and Sonny finally signed a significant contract with the Orleans Parish School Board. It was the plan to do all the distribution themselves, which meant delivering to 115 schools in a single day.

The day before their first delivery was All Saints Day. Good Creole Catholic that he was, Sonny went with his wife and sister Marlene to visit all the relatives' graves in the cemetery that day. He seemed a little flushed, and his sister convinced him to go to the emergency room. Sonny died of a heart attack just outside of Ochsner Hospital.

That was the first time Vance had to take charge alone. He and Sonny had only worked together for seven years, but he knew what he had to do. There were so many people and rental trucks lined up for the next morning's deliveries. My husband went to work and was waiting when the crew arrived. He told everyone Sonny had passed, then together, they loaded the trucks, and the rest is history.

Together, Vance and I have forged our own path for the family business. When Hurricane Katrina wiped out our factory and our home, Vance found a local facility to produce the family's famous sausage so we could all be together in our Jazz Fest booth on opening day 2006, just eight months after Katrina. After all, we come from generations of indomitable people.

Every time we introduce new flavors like jerk chicken and crawfish sausage to our loyal festival fan base, they've clamored for more. Vance's innovations quickly become new po' boy favorites at our booth. At home, I always enjoy playing with ways to turn them into new family dinners.

Creole Crawfish Jambalaya

Yields 8-10 Servings

Since Vaucresson Sausage's earliest days, our Creole hot sausage has always played an important role in jambalaya. Since Vance came up with a recipe for Creole crawfish sausage, this version has become a favorite both in and out of crawfish season. It's so buttery and rich, it combines all the best elements of etouffee and jambalaya in one pot.

2 lbs. Vaucressons Creole Crawfish Sausage
1 onion, chopped
4 stalks celery, chopped
1 bell pepper, chopped
3 tbsp. tomato paste
12 tbsp. butter, divided in half
3 cups long grain white rice
6 cups chicken stock or water
3 cloves garlic, minced
2 tsps. thyme
1 bay leaf
1 tbsp. Creole seasoning
¼ tsp. cayenne pepper
1 lb. crawfish tail
¼ cup thinly sliced green onions
Salt to taste
Hot sauce to taste

Remove the sausage from its casing and sauté until browned, breaking it up into the consistency of ground meat. Add onion, celery, and bell pepper and continue sautéing for about 10 minutes until seasoning vegetables are soft. Stir in tomato paste and cook together with seasoning vegetables for about 5 minutes to enhance tomato paste flavor.

Stir in 4 tbsp. butter. When butter melts, add rice and stir together for 3-4 minutes. Add chicken stock/water, garlic, thyme, bay leaf, Creole seasoning, and black pepper. Bring to a boil, then cover and reduce heat to a low simmer.

Cook without stirring for 25-30 minutes. Using a fork, fluff up rice grains, then stir in remaining 8 tbsp. butter, crawfish tails, and green onions. Cover and cook on low for another 5 minutes. Season to taste with salt and hot sauce and serve.

Black Beans and Jerk Chicken Sausage

Yields 8 servings

Vance and I love to dream up new sausage flavors to entice our customers. After tasting a lot of authentic Jamaican jerk at festivals, we decided a Jerk Chicken Sausage was in order. It's quickly become a customer favorite.

1 lb. Vaucresson's Creole Jerk Chicken Sausage
¼ lb. ham, cubed
1 large onion, chopped
½ green bell pepper, chopped
2 stalks celery, chopped
6 cups water or chicken stock
1 lb. dried black beans, rinsed
1 bay leaf
1 tbsp. garlic powder
1 tbsp. onion powder
½ tsp. thyme
½ tsp. cumin
⅛ tsp. clove
⅛ tsp. allspice
⅛ tsp. nutmeg
1 smoked turkey leg, (if available)
8 cups cooked rice

In a large skillet, brown sausage. Remove from pan and cool. Cut sausage into ¼ inch slices and set aside.

In an 8-qt. stock pot, combine ham, onion, bell pepper, celery, water/chicken stock and dried black beans. Bring to a boil. Add bay leaf and all dried seasonings. Lower to a simmer and cook for 2 ½ hours or more, stirring frequently until beans are tender. Add more water/chicken stock as needed.

Add sliced sausage and smoked turkey wings (if available), then cook for another hour over a medium low heat, stirring frequently until beans are soft and creamy.

Serve over cooked rice.

White Beans with Shrimp and Creole Crawfish Sausage

Yields 8 servings

White beans with shrimp is the seafood alternative to red beans and rice. It was a favorite on Fridays when old Creole customs dictated meatless meals on that day. Vaucresson's Creole Crawfish Sausage does have pork, but it sets my white beans apart from every other.

1 lb. Vaucresson's Creole Crawfish Sausage
1 large onion, chopped
½ green bell pepper, chopped
2 stalks celery, chopped
6 cups water or chicken stock
1 lb. dried white beans, rinsed
1 bay leaf
1½ lbs. small, peeled raw shrimp
¼ cup Italian parsley, chopped
1 tbsp. garlic powder
Creole seasoning to taste
Black pepper to taste
8 cups cooked rice

In a large skillet, brown sausage. Remove from pan and cool. Cut sausage into ¼ inch slices and set aside.

In an 8-qt. stock pot, combine onion, bell pepper, celery, water/chicken stock, dried white beans, and bay leaf. Bring to a boil. Lower to a simmer and cook for 2½ hours or more, stirring frequently until beans are tender. Add more water/chicken stock as needed.

Add sliced sausage, then cook for another hour over a medium low heat stirring frequently until beans are soft and creamy. Add shrimp, parsley, and garlic powder. Cook for 15 minutes. Add Creole seasoning and black pepper to taste.

Serve over cooked rice.

Julie and Vance

CHAPTER FOUR

Let's Get the Party Started!

"Can I get you some drinks or an appetizer to start?" I'm always the one who quickly answers, "Yes!" Appetizers are actually my favorite part of the meal. Often, I'll order two or more. They're fun and made for sharing and mutual enjoyment.

Appetizers help start conversation and are great ice breakers. For me, the appetizer sets the tone for the rest of the meal, and in many cases the whole evening. Many great dates started over chips and queso with margaritas. Shared small plates are a great way to lighten the mood and eliminate awkward voids in conversation. Good food is a bonding experience and sharing food brings a closeness, a special vibe.

I knew my husband Vance was the one for me on our first date. We went to Joe's Crab Shack, and he ordered three appetizers to start. "Yes!" I thought, "I hit the jackpot with this one!" That first date was amazing, perfect even, so much so that I knew I was going to marry him.

Thank God we had that perfect first date because many of our dates that followed weren't so great. Vance and I started dating shortly after his father's sudden death. He had just taken over the family business and moved back home to take care of his mother. His time was limited, and he was usually exhausted, but his intentions were good.

Our frequent dates centered around dinner, always with appetizers and cocktails. I would be working my best look on a date with the man I intended to marry and while sharing some good food, he would fall asleep right there at the table! I had to wonder, "Was it me?" He couldn't possibly think I was boring, could he? If nothing else, it was extremely humbling.

Falling asleep on dates wasn't limited to dinner, Vance did this all the time. At concerts, plays, and even once while we were on the dance floor doing the electric slide. I couldn't decide which was crazier, him falling asleep or me continuing to date him. Once, when I was ready to call it quits, my sister, Angela gave me the best advice. She said, "Julie, he may be a terrible boyfriend,

Julie's bridal shower

but he'll be a great husband. Hang in there!" Angela was right, over twenty years later, we are still going strong.

When I started dating Vance, I was eager to show off my culinary skills. Of course, I was nervous because I assumed that he would have high expectations since he came from a family steeped in New Orleans culinary history. I decided to put any trepidation aside, planned a wonderful dinner, and invited him over.

I remember the details that went into the whole evening. I left work early to grocery shop, carefully selecting each item. Everything needed to be perfect, the food, my outfit, and the table. I wanted it to be special.

I had amazing wine, and my stereo was softly playing the perfect music. The table was set with candles and a beautiful flower arrangement. My menu consisted of a mixed green salad with shaved parmesan cheese and spicy boiled shrimp, followed by panée chicken cutlets fried to a perfect golden brown, juicy and tender. I served the chicken on a bed of tricolor pasta with a delicate crabmeat cream sauce along with a side of freshly shucked corn, sautéed with onions and mixed peppers. For dessert we had white chocolate bread pudding served on a plate drizzled with milk chocolate and garnished with shaved chocolate curls.

Everything went so well. We drank almost two bottles of wine, laughing and talking the whole evening. When he left, Vance declared that was one of the best meals he had ever had. My feet hadn't touched the ground all night because I just knew I had sealed the deal. The food was good, and he actually stayed awake the entire time. I couldn't wait to hear from him again.

The next morning while getting ready for work, I anxiously awaited his call. Vance always called on his way to work. No call came, but I assured myself, "Maybe he's busy this morning. No worries. Surely, I'll hear from him this afternoon." When afternoon arrived and there was still no call I thought, "Well ok, he's probably got a lot going on at work today. They must be making hog's head cheese. It's always a huge production. I'll talk to him this evening."

I went to my jazzercise class but couldn't focus, waiting to hear from him. That day rolled into the next and so on and so on. After three weeks of dead silence, that fool finally decided to call. I was terribly heartbroken and angry, yet I answered the phone. Vance talked like nothing was wrong. I was dumbfounded. He thought we could continue right where we left off. I confronted him, insisting on an explanation. Sheepishly, he explained he blew me off because he was scared. He felt I was the marrying kind, and he wasn't ready for that.

Despite that bump in the road, I invited Vance to come with me to Sunday dinner at Momma's house. As we walked in, he saw the table set with linens and fine china. There were two flower arrangements of bright pink camellias from Momma's garden and a beautiful crystal pitcher filled with her famous punch.

We started with oyster and artichoke soup, followed by roasted turkey with asparagus and parslied potatoes. Vance leaned over to quietly ask me what the occasion was. I casually replied that this was a normal Sunday dinner for us. I could see the light bulb going off. It was then that he realized I wasn't trying to trap him, and I heard him faintly say, "Oh, ok, y'all just eat like this."

That Sunday dinner represented a lot to Vance. Vaucresson Sausage has always stood for Culture, Community and Cuisine—something we call "The 3 C's." When he told his mother he wanted to marry me, she had a "3-C" criteria of her own. Geraldine wanted to know, "Is she Catholic, college-educated, and Creole?" Lucky for me, I'm all three!

The tradition of Sunday dinner leaves lasting impressions on people's psyches as well as their palettes. I believe what we have helped prepare and then consume together, gives us a foundation to appreciate good food that comes from our deep cultural influences.

My bridesmaids, Monique Ally, Michele Fontenot, Julie, Michele Stiaes, and my sister, Angela

Shower Punch

Yields 24 servings

At every shower, we had some variation of the same punch. It was always with sherbet and ginger ale. The flavor of sherbet often varied. Sometimes it was made with Hawaiian Punch and at other times, Sprite. Regardless of the variation, the result was always a punch that teetered on being a dessert.

1 2-liter bottle Hawaiian Punch
1 64-oz. bottle orange juice
1½-gallon orange sherbet
1 2-liter bottle ginger ale

Combine Hawaiian Punch and orange juice in a punch bowl. Spoon the container of sherbet into the bowl with the punch and juice. Slowly pour the ginger ale into the punch bowl to retain the carbonation. Serve over ice.

Chicken Salad

Yields 4 servings

In my family, there is no such thing as just ordering a tray of finger sandwiches. They are strictly made at home, involving loaves of white bread and an electric knife to cut off the crusts and slice the sandwiches into quarters. The chicken is boiled then put through a meat grinder with the celery. The result is a uniquely smooth and creamy chicken salad. Today, I use leftover chicken or bake a few breasts to make a small batch.

2 cups cooked chicken, finely chopped
1 stalk celery, finely chopped
3 green onions, finely chopped
2 tbsp. parsley, chopped
¾ cup mayonnaise
½ tsp. Creole seasoning
½ tsp. black pepper

Combine all the ingredients in a small bowl and mix well.

Serve on sandwich bread, with greens as a salad or with crackers.

Shrimp Mold

Yields 10-12 servings

Creole bridal and baby showers of the past were different than today. There weren't any professional decorations with balloon arches and fancy catering. All the food was prepared by family members and several traditional items were always served. You could always count on having shrimp mold, chicken salad sandwiches, deviled eggs, and punch made with sherbet. Without these old standards, it just wasn't a party.

1 8-oz. Philadelphia cream cheese, softened
1 10-oz. can tomato soup
1 envelope unflavored gelatin
½ cup cold water
2 lbs. cooked shrimp, chopped
¾ cup celery, finely chopped
¾ cup green onion, finely chopped
1 tbsp. Creole seasoning
1 tsp. garlic powder
½ tsp. cayenne pepper
Ritz crackers

In a medium saucepan, melt Philadelphia cream cheese and mix in tomato soup over medium heat, combining thoroughly. Let mixture cool.

Soak gelatin in cold water, then add to the soup and cream cheese mixture. Add the remaining ingredients and mix well. Pour into a mold and refrigerate several hours or overnight until firm.

To unmold, briefly submerge mold in warm water to loosen, being careful not to spill water into the shrimp mold itself. Turn out onto a serving platter.

Serve with Ritz crackers.

CRESSON'S
LE CAFÉ & DELI

Rosalyn Thompson
at the café

Rosalyn's Spicy Crack Pretzels

Yields 16 servings

Just like my friend Rosalyn to come up with the craziest, easiest recipe that people just can't stop eating. Poured straight out of the dry marinade, these pretzels don't appear very different, but the taste is absolutely addictive!

1 16-oz. bag pretzel sticks
1 gallon zip lock baggie
1 tsp. cayenne pepper
1 tsp. lemon pepper seasoning
1½ tsp. granulated garlic
1 package Hidden Valley Ranch dry mix
¾ cup canola oil

Put pretzels in a gallon resealable bag. Mix cayenne pepper, lemon pepper, granulated garlic, ranch dressing mix, and canola oil together. Pour over the pretzels in the baggie. Let sit for at least 2 hours, but it's best if it sits overnight.

Pour into a serving bowl and watch the spicy crack fly!

Our wedding day

Deviled Eggs

Yields 18 eggs

Pickles, olives, and deviled eggs were a staple at every gathering. Most were basically the same, just some had pickle relish, and some didn't. Deviled eggs are making a comeback with all sorts of variations like crab, shrimp, or even bacon bits. I prefer the classic version, *with* sweet relish please.

9 hard-boiled eggs, peeled
⅓ cup mayonnaise
⅓ cup sweet relish
2 tsps. Vaucresson Creole Mustard
Creole seasoning to taste
Black pepper to taste
Paprika for garnish

Cut eggs in half lengthwise, remove the yolks, and place in a medium bowl. Arrange egg whites on a platter.

Mash the yolks with a fork. Add mayonnaise, relish, Creole mustard, Creole seasoning, and pepper. Mix together until smooth. Stuff or pipe filling into the egg halves. Sprinkle with paprika.

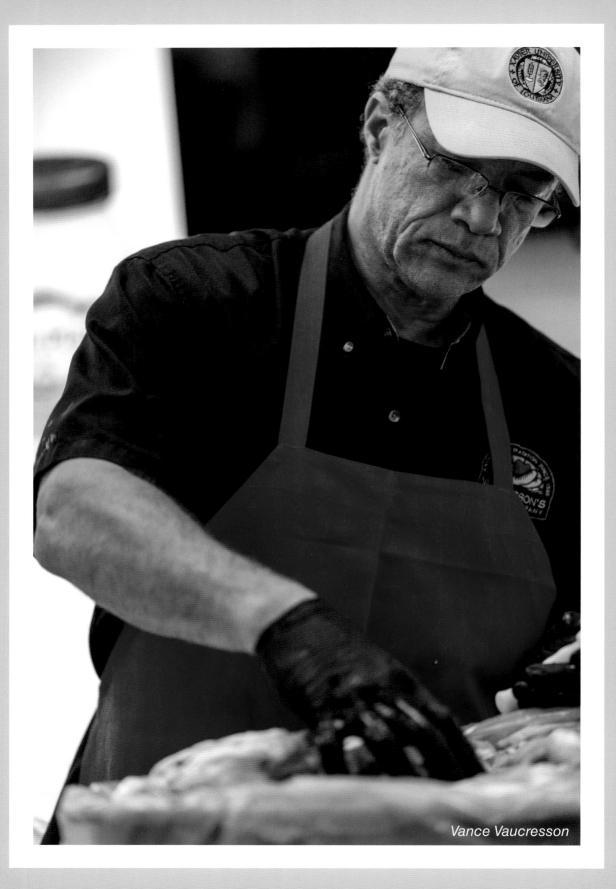

Vance Vaucresson

CHAPTER FIVE

Cooking Outside the Casing

I've always loved to cook. When I started preparing complete meals at twelve, I asked Mom to write down recipes she thought I could handle. She carefully broke everything down for me, making them super easy to follow.

When I started a family of my own, I assumed that it would be a piece of cake since Vance and I only had two kids—huge mistake. It's hard being responsible for everybody and everything. There's a lot of pressure keeping up with lunch accounts, uniforms, appointments, practices, shoes, rehearsals, pajama days—the list goes on and on. All of this has to happen while still managing to work, be a wife, and meet the demands of the never-ending task of meal planning.

When I started to get overwhelmed, I would go to my mother for advice, especially with the daily dilemma of what we should have for dinner. My mother would tell me I was making this way harder than I needed to. She said, "Cooking for your family is about love Julie, don't stress over it. Recipes are just guides. Follow them, but make them your own. If you don't have an ingredient, just use what you do have and make it work."

That helped me stop panicking over things. I started thinking about Momma's words, "Just use what you have," on nights when I hadn't remembered to thaw anything out or had to work late. One of those nights as I gazed into the refrigerator, I realized there was always lots of sausage there. After all, I am married to a third-generation sausage maker.

As I gazed into the fridge, I thought about how I needed to rethink my life, and it hit me; I had to think *outside the casing*. Sausage can be used in so many ways and our Vaucresson sausage is so full of flavor, I quickly discovered when I used it as an ingredient *outside the casing* it always made a delicious dinner easy.

Thinking "outside the casing" has become a metaphor for my life. I have had to "think-outside the casing" to maintain my sanity while trying to be super mom. There's always a way, and if there isn't, I make one. I had to stop having unrealistic expectations that only left me feeling worse when they weren't achieved. Who would have guessed that meal planning could be the epiphany for a major life change that has brought me great happiness? I believe inspiration comes in many forms; we just have to be ready to receive it.

Creole Italian Sausage Stuffed Tomatoes

Yields 6 servings

Creole tomatoes are Louisiana's homegrown favorite. Grown along the banks of the Mississippi River, when they're in season, I love to eat them with nothing but a little salt and pepper. Although any tomatoes can be used for this recipe, Creole tomatoes are clearly the best.

6 large, very firm Creole or other tomatoes
1 lb. Vaucresson Creole Italian Sausage, out of the casing
2 tsps. olive oil
1 medium onion, chopped
1 medium bell pepper, chopped
3-4 cloves garlic, finely chopped
1-2 cups Progresso Italian breadcrumbs
1 cup grated Parmesan cheese
1 cup shredded mozzarella cheese

Preheat oven to 350 degrees.

Slice the tops off the tomatoes and scoop out the pulp into a bowl and set aside.

In a skillet, brown sausage then drain on paper towel to eliminate any excess grease. Add olive oil to the same skillet over a medium heat. Sauté onions and bell peppers until soft. Add the garlic and cook for 3 minutes. Stir in the tomato pulp and simmer together for about 4 minutes, then add the sausage, cooking for an additional 3 minutes. Remove from heat.

Stir in Parmesan cheese and add the breadcrumbs, mixing together until thick enough to stuff the tomatoes.

Stuff the tomatoes and cover each one with the shredded mozzarella cheese. Place in a baking pan and bake 15-20 minutes until mozzarella cheese is melted. Watch carefully to not overbake or the tomatoes will be too soft.

Sausage Hashbrown Casserole

Yields 10 servings

This will forever be my hurricane meal. After Hurricane Ida, my family were all in New Iberia. That included my family of four, my mom, and my brother with his family of five. We all took turns cooking and one day, it was my turn to cook breakfast. We always evacuate with sausage, so I came prepared. I made this casserole, and everyone loved it. It's a comforting dish and can feed a crowd.

1 30-oz. package frozen shredded hashbrowns, thawed
Creole seasoning to taste
Black pepper to taste
4 tsps. butter
1 medium onion, finely chopped
2 lbs. Vaucresson Breakfast Sausage
8 large eggs
2 cups half and half
2 cups shredded cheddar cheese

Preheat oven to 350 degrees and grease a 9x13 casserole dish. Spread hashbrowns in the casserole dish to make a bottom crust and sprinkle with Creole seasoning and black pepper. Bake for 10-15 minutes.

Melt butter in a pan and sauté onions until soft and translucent, then add breakfast sausage and cook for 8-10 minutes. Whisk the eggs and half and half together.

Remove hashbrowns from the oven and layer with cheese, sausage, and then another layer of cheese. Pour the half and half and egg mix evenly over the casserole.

Cover with foil and bake for 30 minutes. Uncover and bake for an additional 15 minutes until the egg mixture has set.

Cut into generous squares and serve.

Creole Sloppy Jeaux

Yields 8 servings

My girlfriends and I often get together to play Pokeno. Each member of the group takes a turn hosting and plans a menu including snacks. When it was my friend Michelle's turn to host, she served Sloppy Joes and we all went crazy. I hadn't had a Sloppy Joe since middle school and was pleasantly surprised how delicious it was. I went home and started thinking how great this would be if I combined our hot sausage with the ground chuck. Vance and the kids all loved it so much, we decided to Creolize "Joe" to Jeaux!

1 lb. ground chuck, seasoned with salt and black pepper to taste
1 lb. Vaucresson Creole Hot Sausage, out of the casing
1 medium onion, chopped
½ green bell pepper, chopped
¼ red bell pepper, chopped
3-4 cloves garlic, finely chopped
1 15-oz. can tomato sauce
2 tbsp. brown sugar
1 tbsp. Vaucresson's Creole Mustard
1 tsp. Lea & Perrins Worcestershire sauce
½ tsp. chili powder
Creole seasoning to taste
Black pepper to taste
8 seeded hamburger buns

Thoroughly combine ground chuck with hot sausage and brown together in a 3-quart sauté pan. Remove from heat and drain any grease. Add onions and peppers to the pan and sauté until soft.

Add garlic and tomato sauce to the pan and cook for about 3-4 minutes.

In a bowl, mix brown sugar, Creole mustard, Worcestershire sauce, and chili powder. Add to the pan with the meats, stirring together well. Simmer for 10 minutes.

Season with Creole seasoning and pepper to taste and serve on hamburger buns with coleslaw on the side.

VAUCRESSON
CAFÉ CREOLE

Phone 523-8437
624 BOURBON STREET
NEW ORLEANS, LOUISIANA

624 Bourbon is a classically lovely Creole building. It stands
with a hipped roof opened by splendid dormers. Alone of its kind, it
other building in its block.

Built in 1814 by young Dr. Fortin for his bride, Amenaide, its
opens into a carriage drive that leads back to a deep courtyard. Origi
two other openings here. Luxuriously arched, these contained Frenc
transoms. Years ago the arches were altered and narrower windows o
place.

SPECIALIZING IN THE CREOLE CUISINE FOR WHICH NEW OR

CHAPTER SIX

Vaucresson's Café Creole

Of all Sonny's ventures, Vaucresson's Café Creole is perhaps the most storied. Located in the French Quarter, it was the first business since Reconstruction to be owned by a person of color on world famous Bourbon Street. In his previous business dealings, Sonny had made a name for himself among the Quarter's powerbrokers of the day. Despite his very fair skin and brilliant blue eyes, Sonny never intentionally used his looks to "pass" as White. When people got to know Sonny, they knew the man himself, not necessarily labeled as a Black man or a Creole.

Sonny's partner in Vaucresson's Café Creole was Larry Borenstein, who is known as the father of Preservation Hall. Despite the approval of many prominent Quarter businessmen, in the turbulent racial climate of the day there was pushback. A meeting of the Bourbon Street Merchants Association buzzed with hushed talk about how "one of those people" was coming to Bourbon Street and would bring down property values and invite more of "that element" into the Quarter.

Sonny loved to tell the story of that association meeting. One of the businessmen sat down with him and Borenstein and said, "I'm just so upset that this guy is coming—I just can't believe this." Borenstein spoke up, "I know the guy. I'll introduce you." He gestured towards Sonny saying, "You know Sonny?" "Of course, I know Sonny! I just shook hands with him and gave him a hug when I came in," the man replied. "Well, he's the new n word on Bourbon Street," Borenstein explained. Sonny always laughed remembering how "The guy turned pale white, began to sweat, and got up from the table and left." With the full blessing of the Merchants Association, Vaucresson's Café Creole opened at 624 Bourbon Street.

FAMOUS

Calas

Yields 12 calas

Calas are old school New Orleans sweet rice fritters. Long before the Civil War, many slave women were given a day off on Sunday. They would make calas, a rice cake originally from Ghana and Liberia and sell them in the streets. Walking through the French Quarter with baskets on their head they called out, *"Belle calas! Tout chaud!"* which means, "Beautiful calas! Very hot!" Calas later became a treat served on very special family occasions. It was a Catholic Creole tradition to serve calas when children made their first communion.

2 cups cooked rice, cooled
6 tbsp. all-purpose flour
3 tbsp. sugar
2 tsp. baking powder
¼ tsp. salt
¼ tsp. vanilla
2 eggs
4 cups vegetable oil for frying
½ cup confectioner's sugar

In a large bowl, mix rice, flour, sugar, baking powder, and salt. Sprinkle vanilla on top and mix well. Add eggs and combine thoroughly.

Heat vegetable oil in a 5-quart pot to 360 degrees. Using two large tbsp., form calas by moving from one spoon to another before dropping into oil. Fry until browned on both sides.

Drain on paper towel and sprinkle with powdered sugar. Serve hot.

Café au Lait

The secret to real café au lait is freshly dripped, strong black coffee with chicory, combined with equal parts whole milk, heated to a near boil. True café au lait is made using both hands, pouring the coffee and the milk simultaneously into a cup, creating a slightly foamy top. A cup of café au lait at Vaucresson's Café Creole was served for just 40 cents.

Banana Fritters

Yield 12

My mother-in-law's family worked for the Vaccaro family. The Vaccaro family owned Standard Fruit Company, importing bananas from Honduras to New Orleans. Geraldine said she had so many bananas growing up, she never wanted to see one again. That didn't last long, because banana fritters were featured on the Vaucresson's Café Creole menu, 3 for 75 cents.

1 very ripe banana, mashed
¼ cup milk
1 cup all-purpose flour
1½ tsp. baking powder
¼ tsp. salt
1 egg, beaten
1 tbsp. butter, melted
4 cups vegetable oil for frying
¼ cup confectioners' sugar

In a large mixing bowl, combine banana and milk. Combine flour, baking powder, and salt and sift over banana mixture. Add eggs and melted butter, mixing together thoroughly.

In a heavy pot, heat oil to 360 degrees. Drop batter by the tbsp. fully into the oil and fry until lightly browned.

Drain on paper towel. Serve hot sprinkled with confectioners' sugar.

Creole Biscuits

Yields 1 dozen biscuits

My mom made biscuits from scratch every weekend when we were growing up. On Saturday we would have her biscuits, and on Sunday mornings we had buttermilk drops from McKenzie's. We loved breakfast on the weekends. If I had to decide on a favorite, mom's homemade biscuits and her egg sandwiches would be a close tie. These two breakfast items were legendary in our family. I still enjoy a good biscuit made from scratch. Vaucresson's Café Creole sold Creole biscuits for 30 cents.

1 cup shortening
2 cups sifted flour
1 tsp. salt
½ tsp. cream of tartar
4 tsp. baking powder
¾ to 1 cup milk

Preheat oven to 450 degrees.

Mix shortening with the sifted dry ingredients. Gradually add milk to form a soft dough. Knead for 1 minute on a lightly floured surface. Roll out to a ½ inch thickness. Cut with a floured biscuit cutter. Place on a greased baking sheet. Bake at 450 degrees for 12-15 minutes.

Pain Perdu

Serves 4

Pain perdu, or lost bread, is French toast made with French bread. Buttery and sweet, at home we serve ours with both powdered sugar and cane syrup.

2 eggs
1 cup whole milk
2 tbsp. sugar
1 tsp. vanilla
12 slices of stale po' boy bread, ½ inch thick
4 tbsp. butter
½ cup confectioner's sugar
Cane syrup

Mix eggs, milk, sugar, and vanilla, combining well.

Melt butter in a 12-inch frying pan. Dip po' boy bread into egg mixture, soaking thoroughly. Brown pain perdu on each side.

Serve sprinkled with powdered sugar and cane syrup on the side.

Omelette Paysanne

Yields 1 serving

We loved going to the Hotel Intercontinental for their Mother's Day brunch. The kids would be fascinated with all the varieties of food displayed at all the different stations. My son VJ's first stop was always the omelette station. He loved being able to choose what would go inside, always picking different cheeses, veggies, and sausage. Omelette Paysanne means peasant omelette and was a mainstay at Vaucresson's Café Creole.

1 tbsp. butter
¼ onion, diced
¼ cup diced Idaho potatoes, cooked
¼ tsp. cayenne pepper
⅛ tsp. salt
¼ tsp. Italian parsley, chopped

Melt butter in a 10-inch nonstick omelette pan. Add onion and sauté over medium heat until translucent. Stir in the potatoes and season with cayenne and salt. Pour eggs over the potato and onion mixture, continuously shaking the pan to allow eggs to set. Periodically, lift an edge and tilt the pan to allow uncooked eggs to run under omelette and set. When eggs are cooked, transfer omelette from pan to plate, folding into thirds.

Sprinkle with fresh parsley and serve at once.

Omelette Chaurice

Yields 1 serving

Chaurice and eggs go together like Julie and Vance. The chaurice omelette made at Vaucresson's Café Creole was a popular showcase for our family's famous hot sausage.

1 tbsp. butter
3 eggs, beaten
¼ cup Vaucresson Chaurice Sausage, browned
¼ tsp. Italian parsley, chopped

Melt butter in a 10-inch omelette pan. Add eggs and shake constantly until they set. Periodically, tilt pan allowing uncooked eggs to run under omelette and set.

Sprinkle sausage on the omelette and fold in half. Sprinkle with fresh parsley and serve at once.

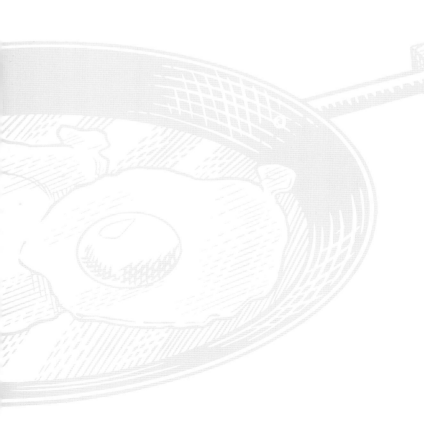

Breakfast Menu

No. 1   1 Egg, Toast, Orange Juice & Coffee *110*

No. 2   Two Eggs, Toast, Orange Juice & Coffee *140*

No. 3   Two Eggs, Toast, Orange Juice & Coffee

Choice of:

Bacon, Ham, Sausage Pattie or Chaurice *170*

No. 4   1 Egg, Toast, Orange Juice & Coffee

Choice of:

Ham, Bacon, Sausage Pattie or Chaurice *160*

No. 5   Creole Breakfast

Liver - Grits - 2 Eggs - Biscuits or Toast *270*

No. 6   Breakfast Steak

2 Eggs - Hash Brown - Toast - Coffee *270*

Omelettes   *Served with Toast and Butter*

Plain Omelette *160*

Cheese Omelette *180*

Omelette Paysenne *(Ham and Onions)* *190*

Chaurice Omelette *(Our Special Hot Sausage)* *190*

Omelette Confiture *(Made With Jam)* *175*

Western Omelette *195*

Spanish Omelette *195*

Ala Carte

Hash Brown Potatoes *40*

Order of Toast *30*

Grits *30*

Creole Biscuits *30*

3 Calas *(Little Rice Cakes, from old Creole Recipe)* *75*

Lost Bread *(2 pieces of French Bread dipped in Batter and Fried)* *75*

3 Fritters (Plain or Banana)
(Small Batter Cakes that are Fried) *75*

Order of Sausage Patties

Chaurice, Ham or Bacon *75*
Butter and Jam served with Toast and Biscuits

Liver and Onions

Yields 4 servings

The Creole Breakfast, which consisted of liver, grits, two eggs with biscuits or toast was a popular meal at Vaucresson's Café Creole. Hearty and delicious, it was ordered by many. The star of this breakfast was the liver. There is nothing like the smell of liver and onions cooking. My older brother Rivers loves liver and onions with grits. My mother didn't make it often but when she did, my brother was always first in line.

1 lb. calves' liver, thinly sliced
4 slices bacon
¼ cup all-purpose flour
¼ tsp. Creole seasoning
¼ cup vegetable oil
4 tbsp. butter
2 large onions, thickly sliced
¼ cup beef stock or water
2 tsp. Lea & Perrins Worcestershire sauce

Remove any membranes from liver and discard. In a 3-quart sauté pan, cook bacon until browned and crispy. Remove bacon from pan, leaving bacon grease in sauté pan.

Combine flour and Creole seasoning. Add vegetable oil to reserved bacon grease in sauté pan and heat to medium temperature. Lightly dredge liver in seasoned flour. Brown on each side in sauté pan. Reserve browned liver.

Melt butter in same sauté pan and add onions. Sauté over medium heat for 2-3 minutes, then reduce heat and cover pan. Stir periodically until onions are translucent. Remove onions from sauté pan and reserve.

Add 1 tsp. of dredging flour to sauté pan and stir over medium heat until lightly browned. Make a gravy by whisking in beef stock/water and Worcestershire sauce, stirring up any bits stuck to the pan. Add liver to the gravy, top with sautéed onions, and cover. Cook over a low heat until gravy thickens.

To serve, top each slice of liver with onions and a piece of bacon. Serve with grits.

Les Repas

Steaks *Served with Potatoes and Salad*

BABY BEEF PORTERHOUSE 6.50

VEAL WHOLE SIRLOIN 5.50

HEAVY BEEF LOIN STRIP 7.50

Seafood *Served with Cole Slaw and Potatoes*

FRIED SHRIMP PLATE 2.95

OYSTER PLATE ½ doz. $ 3.00   1 doz. $ 4.00

STUFFED CRAB 2.00

STUFFED SHRIMP 3.25

FILE GUMBO 1.75

SEAFOOD PLATTER 4.50

Sandwiches

HAM & EGG 1.50   2.25

HAM 1.25   2.25

OYSTER 2.00   3.00

PANEE' MEAT 1.50   2.75

HAM & CHEESE 1.50   2.25

HAMBURGER 85   1.90

CHAURICE 1.25   2.25

CHEESEBURGER 1.25   2.25

ROAST BEEF 1.50   2.50

TROUT 1.50   2.50

SHRIMP 1.50   2.50

WESTERN SAND 1.50   2.50

Beverages

COFFEE 30

TEA OR MILK 35

CAFE AU LAIT 40

LEMONADE 40

HOT CHOCOLATE 40

Panné Meat

Serves 4

Originally, the meat used for panné was always veal because it was so cheap. These days veal is so expensive, it's more often made with pork or chicken. Vance loves panné meat. It was one of the first meals I ever cooked for him. His preference is veal but will take any one of them as long as it's pannéd.

4 large veal or beef cutlets, totaling 1½-2 lbs.
½ cup flour
¼ tsp. salt
⅛ tsp. black pepper
1 egg
½ cup whole milk
1 cup dry breadcrumbs
¼ cup vegetable oil

Pound each cutlet to a thickness of ¼ inch or less, increasing size substantially.

Season flour with salt and pepper. In a pie pan or shallow dish, combine egg and milk. Dredge each cutlet in seasoned flour then dip into egg wash and dredge in breadcrumbs. Heat oil in a heavy skillet over a medium heat. Brown the cutlets on each side and serve.

Stuffed Crab

Serves 6

Stuffed crabs have always been a favorite of mine. I can remember my mom making stuffed crab using crab shell shaped tins. She always served certain special sides with her standard meals. Mom's stuffed crabs were always accompanied by potato salad and sweet peas. If I don't serve it the same way, the meal feels like something is missing. Now I sometimes see stuffed crabs made with actual crab shells, but something about those tin shells makes it feel more authentic to me. Stuffed crabs were also on the menu at Vaucresson's Café Creole, but theirs was served with coleslaw and fried potatoes.

8 tbsp. butter
3 tbsp. onion, finely chopped
6 green onions, thinly sliced
2 celery stalks, finely chopped
1 tbsp. parsley, finely chopped
1 lb. fresh claw crabmeat
½ loaf po' boy bread
¼-½ cup water, depending on dryness of bread
1 cup plain, dry bread crumbs
¼ tsp. salt
⅛ tsp. black pepper

Melt 4 tbsp. butter in a 3-quart sauté pan. Add onion, green onions, celery, and parsley and sauté together for 10 minutes, until soft. Stir in crabmeat and remove from heat.

Thoroughly moisten French bread with water. Chop it finely into a pulp. Mix into the crab mixture. Add salt and black pepper, and dry breadcrumbs as needed. The stuffing should not feel sticky, and it should hold together well.

Fill shells with crab stuffing, sprinkle with additional dried breadcrumbs and dot with remaining butter. Bake at 325 degrees for approximately 25 minutes, until lightly browned.

Stuffed Shrimp

Serves 6

My kids are crazy about stuffed shrimp. It isn't something that I typically cook, so whenever it's on the menu, they order it. They also fight over the leftovers, making sure to write their names on the containers so there is no confusion about what belongs to who. Daddy is known to eat anything that is leftover, so names on the outside are a must! At Vaucresson's Café Creole it came with coleslaw and fried potatoes.

Stuffing
3 tbsp. butter
3 tbsp. onion, finely chopped
2 green onions, thinly sliced
2 tbsp. celery, finely chopped
1 tbsp. flat leaf parsley, finely chopped
1 lb. fresh claw crabmeat
½ loaf po' boy bread
2 eggs, beaten
4 cups plain, dry bread crumbs

36 large raw shrimp
Salt to taste
Black pepper to taste
2 cups plain flour
1 cup milk
1 egg
4 cups vegetable oil for frying

Melt butter in a 3-quart sauté pan. Add the onion, green onions, celery, and parsley. Sauté together for 10 minutes, until soft. Add crabmeat and sauté for another 5 minutes. Moisten French bread with water thoroughly. Chop it finely into a pulp. Stir in eggs. Add crabmeat to egg and bread mixture, mixing well. Add 2–3 tbsp. of the dry breadcrumbs, until stuffing is no longer sticky to the touch.

Peel shrimp, leaving tails on. Butterfly each shrimp and stuff with approximately 1 tbsp. of filling. Season flour with salt and pepper. In a pie pan or shallow dish, mix milk and egg together to make an egg wash. Roll each stuffed shrimp in flour, egg wash, and then breadcrumbs.

In a deep skillet, heat oil to 375 degrees and fry shrimp for about 5 minutes, until browned. Drain on paper towel and serve.

Hush Puppies

Yields 24 servings

Hush puppies are a side item staple at many New Orleans seafood restaurants. My mom used to make these for us as a snack. The joke was we would burn our tongues eating them right out of the grease, but we couldn't stop. Hush puppies are so good they deserve to be more than a side on a seafood platter.

½ **cup flour, sifted**
1 cup cornmeal
1½ tsp. baking powder
1 tsp. Creole seasoning
1 tsp. sugar
1 small onion, minced
1 egg
½ **cup milk**
Oil for frying

Mix flour, cornmeal, baking powder, Creole seasoning, and sugar. Stir in onion and egg. Slowly add milk to make a stiff dough.

In a deep, heavy pot, heat oil to 365 degrees. Drop teaspoonfuls of hush puppy mix into the hot oil and fry until golden brown, approximately 3-5 minutes. Drain on paper towel.

Serve at once, or hold in a warm oven until ready to serve.

CHAPTER SEVEN

Rebirth of Vaucresson's Creole Café and Deli

My husband, Vance, and I were determined to open our own Vaucresson's Creole Café and Deli right on the same Seventh Ward corner of St. Bernard Avenue and North Roman where Sonny established his Vaucresson sausage business.

Countless people share fond memories of frequenting that corner when my father-in-law Sonny ran a processing facility with a small retail outlet there. I remember going with my mother when I was a little girl to see Mr. Sonny and get that special, hot sausage. It was usually right after a trip to the Circle Food Store to pick up bell peppers on sale, five for a dollar.

I never met my father-in-law, but I feel like I know him from the countless heartwarming stories I hear. Sonny never met a stranger and would always give a little "lagniappe," that New Orleans tradition of tucking a little something extra in. People loved that.

For eighteen long years, since Hurricane Katrina, my husband had been trying to get back on that corner. After overcoming multiple financial roadblocks, we were finally moving right along with our reopening plans when the pandemic hit. With our wholesale customers gone overnight, we were forced to rethink our business model. Instead of relying heavily on institutional sales, we had to pivot and start selling direct-to-consumer. Since the café hadn't opened, we didn't have a retail customer base yet. I figured if we wanted to sell more sausage, we had to show people what they can do with it. Vaucresson sausage is for so much more than just gumbo, red beans, or a hot sausage po' boy.

It was my turn to stand up and help the family business. I virtually turned my apron into a cape to make things happen Supermom style. That's how my alter ego, Julie V, was born. I started creating easy-to-follow recipes featuring different varieties of our sausage.

I never liked recipes with a ton of ingredients, and I don't want to buy special spices I might never use again. I wanted to show other working folks like us, no matter how busy you are, you can prepare good food in easy ways. Our sausage does most of the work for you, easily delivering that authentic Creole flavor.

Luckily, I got a call from our local, Fox 8 News, asking if I'd come cook some easy, fast sausage recipes on their noon broadcast. Supermom, Julie V quickly gained a following and I became a regular on the broadcast, a great way to show people how to "think outside the casing" using Vaucresson Sausage. It really *is* "Creole Made Easy."

It's always good to hear that our food reminds someone of their own family's cooking traditions. One day when I had stuffed peppers for a Fox 8 broadcast, the whole staff came back to the kitchen to taste them. The front receptionist declared that the smell of the peppers in the air and their taste in her mouth brought back her grandmother's cooking. When the smell or taste of good food evokes a positive memory, it is the ultimate thrill for me as a cook. Having what you serve compared to the great cooking of someone's beloved ancestors is truly the best compliment.

On the Fox 8 News set

Hot Sausage and Red Bean Dip

Yields 12 servings

I got a call to appear on the local Fox 8 affiliate to show viewers how to use their New Year's Day leftovers. Vance and I had been on the local news together many times, but this was my first solo appearance. I was so nervous and spent many hours researching and recipe testing. I finally decided on two dishes, cabbage and black-eyed pea stuffed corn bread muffins and black-eyed pea and sausage dip. I have made this dip again and again using black-eyed peas, white beans, and red beans and all are delicious.

1 lb. Vaucresson Hot Sausage, out of the casing
1 8-oz. package cream cheese
2 cups leftover red beans
2 cups sharp cheddar cheese
15½-oz. bag Frito Scoops

Brown sausage and drain any excess grease.

Melt cream cheese in a saucepan. Add hot sausage and mix well. Mix in leftover beans.

Put in a baking dish and top with cheddar cheese. Bake at 350 degrees for 15 minutes until cheese is melted.

Serve with Frito Scoops.

Sausage and Corn Dip

Yields 16 servings

I am the star of every potluck when I bring this dip. It's the perfect complement for socializing and chatting, especially when enjoying a cold margarita.

1 lb. Vaucresson's Hot Sausage, out of the casing
2 8-oz. blocks Philadelphia cream cheese
1 10-oz. can Rotel with green chilis
1 10-oz can corn, drained
2 7-oz cans Mexicorn, drained
1 15-oz. can black beans, rinsed and drained
1 tbsp. taco seasoning
1 cup cheddar cheese, shredded
½ cup Monterrey Jack cheese, shredded
Jalapeños for garnish
Black olives for garnish
Sour cream for garnish
Fritos Scoops or tortilla chips

Preheat oven to 350 degrees.

In a heavy skillet, brown sausage, then drain off excess grease. Add cream cheese and melt over medium heat stirring to mix well. Stir in Rotel, corn, Mexicorn, black beans, and taco seasoning.

Place in an oven safe dish and top with cheddar and Monterrey Jack cheeses. Bake for 10-20 minutes.

Garnish with jalapeños, black olives, and sour cream. Serve with Frito Scoops or tortilla chips.

Hot Sausage Balls

Yields about 4 dozen balls

These hot sausage balls are the epitome of Creole made easy. Just three simple ingredients, these treats are easy to prepare and are a perfect snack.

1 lb. Vaucresson's Creole Hot Sausage, out of the casing
1 cup shredded cheddar cheese, room temperature
3 cups Bisquick

Preheat oven to 350 degrees.

Put hot sausage, cheese, and Bisquick in a large bowl and mix by hand until well combined.

Shape into 1-inch balls. Arrange the balls about 1 inch apart on ungreased baking sheets. Bake until cooked through and browned, about 12-15 minutes. Serve hot.

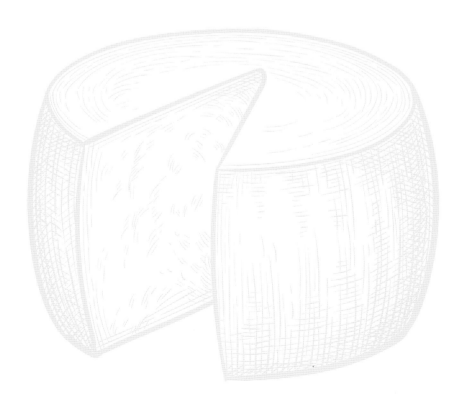

Cornbread Stuffing Bites

Yields 15 1-inch balls

Cornbread stuffing bites are like hush puppies on steroids. If you love cornbread stuffing, these little bites of goodness will be your favorite appetizer.

1 lb. Vaucresson's Creole hot sausage, out of the casing
8 slices cooked bacon, chopped
¼ cup green onions, finely chopped
1 box Jiffy cornbread, prepared according to package directions, crumbled
4 tsps. butter, melted
3 cups shredded sharp cheddar cheese

Preheat oven to 350 degrees.

Brown sausage and drain off any grease and cool.

In a large bowl, mix sausage, bacon, green onions, cornbread, butter, and cheese until thoroughly combined.

Roll into 1-inch balls, packing tightly. Place balls on a parchment lined baking sheet. Bake for 20 minutes. Best served warm.

Creole Hot Sausage Mac & Cheese

Yields 8 servings

We love macaroni and cheese so much, it's a favorite side for many of our meals. During the summer when we're grilling, we often elevate it with our Creole hot sausage. Family and guests now request this spicy twist on the classic whenever we're bringing a dish to a gathering.

1 16-oz. package large elbow noodles
1 lb. Vaucresson Creole Hot Sausage, out of the casing
4 tbsp. butter
¼ cup all-purpose flour
2 cups half and half
1 cup shredded Colby cheese
1 cup shredded sharp cheddar cheese
1 cup shredded mild cheddar cheese, divided in half
Creole seasoning to taste

Preheat oven to 350 degrees.

Boil pasta in salted water till tender. Drain and reserve.

In a heavy skillet, brown the sausage and drain on paper towel. Reserve 2 tbsp. of sausage.

Melt butter in same skillet over medium heat. Whisk in flour, stirring constantly until light golden brown, being careful not to overcook. Add the half and half and mix well. Stir in Colby, sharp cheddar, and half of the mild cheddar cheese, combining until evenly melted.

Mix the pasta and hot sausage together and add to a 9x13 inch buttered casserole pan. Pour the sauce over the macaroni and sausage. Stir to combine well.

Sprinkle the remaining mild cheddar on top and cover with foil. Bake at 350 degrees for 30 minutes. Remove foil and bake uncovered for an additional 15 minutes.

Garnish with 2 tbsp. reserved hot sausage.

*This recipe works perfectly without hot sausage for meatless occasions.

Simonne's Stuffed Bell Peppers

Yields 16 servings

Stuffed bell peppers have been a staple in Creole households for generations. Simonne Glapion Robinson is my godmother, who I affectionately call Nanny. She shared this special recipe with me. She is a phenomenal cook with a Creole cooking style combined with unique elements from New Iberia where my mother's family comes from. Nanny once told me a story about how when she first got married, she asked her mother for a recipe. In that recipe, one of the ingredients called for "a nice piece of meat." Not having any idea what that meant, Nanny asked her mom, "What is a nice piece of meat?" She replied that she should ask the butcher, he'll know what you mean. Nanny and my New Iberia family were some of the best cooks I've ever known. I'm grateful to have had the opportunity to learn from them.

Thank you, Nanny, for always being there when I need you.

1 tbsp. vegetable oil
10 medium green bell peppers, 8 to stuff and 2 chopped for seasoning
2 medium onions, chopped
¼ cup Italian parsley
6 cloves garlic, minced
1 lb. Vaucresson Breakfast Sausage, out of the casing
2 lbs. ground chuck, pork, veal mix
Creole seasoning to taste
Black pepper to taste
1 lb. small shrimp, peeled and deveined
½ tsp. liquid crab boil
8 tbsp. butter
1 cup plain breadcrumbs
1 egg, beaten well
¼ cup breadcrumbs for topping

Heat oil in a large saucepan over medium heat. Add chopped bell pepper, onion, parsley, and garlic. Sauté seasoning for 3-5 minutes. Crumble in breakfast sausage ⅓ at a time, breaking into the consistency of ground meat while mixing with the seasoning.

Season the beef, pork, and veal with Creole seasoning and black pepper. Add to the sausage and seasonings. Reduce heat to medium low and cook together for 10-15 minutes.

Add shrimp to the meat mixture and add the crab boil. Mix well and cook for about 15 minutes.

Turn off heat and add butter, breadcrumbs, and egg. Mix well and add Creole seasoning and pepper if needed and set aside.

Cut peppers in half and clean out seeds and membrane. Stuff each pepper generously with meat mixture and lightly sprinkle with breadcrumbs. Place stuffed peppers in a baking pan.

Add a small amount of water to the bottom of the pan, cover with aluminum foil and bake at 350 degrees for 30-45 minutes or until peppers are tender and the stuffing is browned.

*It's recommended to cook these peppers a day or two ahead of time, refrigerating them until ready to serve. This allows the flavors to marry. They also freeze well.

VAUCRESSON SAUSAGE CO
HOT SAUSAGE
PO-BOY
CRAWFISH SAUSAGE
PO-BOY
ALLIGATOR
Line
3

CHAPTER EIGHT

Festival Season— That Most Wonderful Time of Year

Whew chile . . . April. I have a love/hate relationship with the entire month. During April, everything stops for us as we go into full on festival mode. There's literally no time for anything else. When we aren't at the festival, we're preparing for the festival. Sometimes it seems my marriage vows were to "Love, Honor, and Work Jazz Fest."

Working festivals is a grueling, all-consuming family affair. It's all hands-on deck with our extended family and friends picking up the slack and pitching in. When it comes to having a booth at our biggest annual events, the French Quarter Festival and the New Orleans Jazz and Heritage Festival, it truly takes a village.

I love the role my family plays in this important part of New Orleans culture. Vaucresson Sausage Company is one of the original vendors at the French Quarter Festival and the only one still at Jazz Fest. Our customers love seeing all the family working the booth together every year. Countless people make us their first stop when they hit the festival grounds. Jazz Fest is all about tradition and it's wonderful to know that we are such an important part of so many visitors' personal fest traditions.

The most special part is hearing stories about my father-in-law, Sonny Vaucresson. Unfortunately, I didn't have the opportunity to meet Sonny. He passed away before my husband and I started dating, but I feel like I know him because the legend of Sonny is larger than life.

It is undisputed New Orleans history that the New Orleans Jazz Festival was born at Sonny's Vaucresson Café Creole. Over lunch one day with his business partner, Larry Borenstein and friends, George Wein and Alan Jaffe, the group collectively wondered why the birthplace of jazz couldn't have its own festival like Newport. Wein had founded that successful festival, and it was growing. As the plan developed, someone suggested Sonny could bring food from the café to feed festival goers.

Jazz and Heritage Festival crowd

Sonny was there at Congo Square for that first New Orleans Jazz Festival in 1970 with hot sausage po' boys, wrapped in foil and carried over from the family's restaurant. He loved to talk about Vance's mom, Geraldine showing up with Vance in her arms.

Those early years were tough. Sometimes there were more musicians than visitors, but Sonny remained loyally committed to the festival. His devotion paid off in 1976 when *New York Times* food critic, Mimi Sheraton came to the festival to judge what the newspaper dubbed the "Food Olympics." Sheraton proclaimed Vaucresson's hot sausage po' boys the "very best food at the Fest," cementing its fame forever. It means so much to us to own that special piece of New Orleans food history.

We've watched our kids, Vance Jr., or VJ as he's called, and his sister Hilary grow up at festivals. When they were little, we always brought home treats from the festival for them. As soon as they were able, they were there in the booth with us too. When they were little, it made me laugh to hear them comparing their favorite Fest foods, planning what they'd eat each day. Now they're grown, it's fantastic to watch them actually run the booth by themselves sometimes. I see in them the future of our family business. They are truly keepers of the flame.

Vance and VJ in the booth

Stuffed Artichokes

Yields 6 servings

Every year at Jazz Fest, I look forward to a stuffed artichoke from Vucinovich's, another long-time vendor there. Our booths are at opposite ends of Food Area 1, so it's not always easy for me to get down to theirs. I love Vucinovich's stuffed artichokes so much that I started making my own at home.

6 small artichokes
⅓ cup olive oil and additional for basting
12 cloves garlic, chopped
2 cups Progresso Italian breadcrumbs
½ cup grated Parmesan cheese
4 tbsp. parsley, chopped
½ tsp. Creole seasoning
¼ tsp. black pepper
⅛ tsp. hot sauce

Trim stems from artichokes and remove any damaged leaves. Trim the thorny, upper edges off the leaves. Gently open and separate the leaves. Wash the artichokes and let dry.

In a saucepan, heat olive oil over a medium heat. Add garlic, cooking for 3 minutes and stirring constantly. Remove from heat. Stir in breadcrumbs, Parmesan cheese, parsley, Creole seasoning, black pepper, and hot sauce.

Stuff each leaf with the bread crumb mixture. Place artichokes in a large saucepan with 2 inches of water and cover. Steam over low heat for 1 hour, checking frequently to be sure the pot doesn't boil dry. Baste with olive oil during the cooking. Serve warm.

Stuffed artichokes can be wrapped and frozen for future use. Reheat in aluminum foil.

Corn Pudding

Yields 8 servings

The Crescent City Blues and Barbeque Festival is a fall event produced by the Jazz and Heritage Foundation. It takes place in the New Orleans Central Business District at Lafayette Square, across from Gallier Hall. Vaucresson's hot sausage po' boys have been featured from the very start. One year, our booth was next to a restaurant serving barbeque ribs, smoky greens, and corn pudding. That was the first time I ever tasted corn pudding, and I simply loved it. I ate that dish the whole weekend and after the festival, I was determined to recreate it at home. After a couple of attempts, mine was almost like theirs—but even better!

¼ cup white sugar
3 tbsp. white flour
2 tsp. baking powder
1 tsp. Creole seasoning
6 large eggs
2 cups heavy whipping cream
½ cup salted butter, melted
6 cups yellow corn, fresh, frozen or canned

Combine the sugar, flour, baking powder, and Creole seasoning. Whisk the eggs, heavy whipping cream, and butter together until well blended. Slowly whisk the dry ingredients into the wet ingredients, mixing until smooth. Add the corn and mix well. Pour the mixture into a 9x13-inch baking dish and bake at 350 degrees for 45 minutes. Serve warm.

Crawfish Hilary

Yields 6 servings

The New Orleans Jazz and Heritage Festival is a huge part of our lives. From the last week of April through the first week of May, we spend all time either preparing for it or working our festival booth. Everyone in the family has their favorite festival dishes but for both of my kids, it's always been Crawfish Monica®. Crawfish Monica® is another Jazz Fest standard, created by Pete Hilzim and named for his wife, Monica. VJ and Hilary eat it every day at the Fest. Then, they started requesting it at home. I developed my own version with a Vaucresson twist we call Crawfish Hilary.

1 lb. rotini pasta
8 tbsp. butter
1 medium onion, finely chopped
3 cloves garlic, minced
2 cups heavy cream
2 lbs. fresh, Louisiana crawfish tails
¼ cup parsley, chopped
2 tbsp. River Road Seafood Pasta Seasoning*
Creole seasoning to taste
Cayenne pepper to taste
2 tbsp. garlic powder
¼ cup green onions, chopped

Prepare pasta according to the package and set aside.

In a large saucepan, melt butter over medium heat. Add onions and sauté until soft.

Add the garlic and sauté for 3-4 minutes. Add the heavy cream, stirring well.

Add the crawfish tails and parsley. Cook for 8 minutes, being careful not to overcook.

Add River Road Seafood Pasta seasoning, Creole seasoning, cayenne, and garlic powder.

Mix with rotini pasta and serve garnished with green onions.

*River Road Seafood Pasta Seasoning has just the flavor needed for perfect crawfish pasta. It's widely available online.

CHAPTER NINE

Family Life

Because I work, run around with my kids, and basically manage everything for everybody during the week, I tend to cook casseroles, or one pot meals. Sunday dinner is a totally different deal. It's always something special. Sunday dinner is so much more than just the meal itself. It's about gathering with the people you love and eating together. Sunday dinner is always something we wouldn't eat during the week. No tacos or spaghetti, it's roast with a rich gravy or turkey breast with cornbread stuffing. Sunday dinner takes more time to prepare and always costs more than weekday meals like Monday's red beans and rice. Sunday dinner needs to be a complete meal with multiple sides like a mini holiday celebration.

During the week, my life is so crazy it's hard to come up with different ideas for dinner. My kids don't really consider what my day could have been like. As soon as I hit the door they want to know, "What's for dinner?"

Who knew meal planning would be so hard? I spend a ridiculous amount of time obsessed with that activity. I wake up thinking about what's for dinner. I try my best to plan in advance, but I'm one of those shoppers who buys what looks fresh and tasty.

Do I have to go to the store? Should I thaw something out? Am I working late and need to use the crock pot? All these thoughts race through my head. The worst part of it all are my in-house food critics with their super high expectations. They want a delicious gourmet meal with few leftovers or repeated meals.

I get so burned out trying to come up with ideas of what to cook next that I started a weekly family game. We all write two meals that we would like to have that week on individual slips of paper, allowing for two take-out items like pizza or burgers. Then, we pull for the week's seven meals. The rules are you can't complain about what is chosen, and you can't put anything ridiculous in.

The ridiculous rule began after my daughter, Hilary would write outlandish things like fondue, lobster, and charbroiled oysters. Luckily, these days I have some help with dinner because they have learned to cook some of their favorites, which has been liberating to say the least.

The one time of year there's little debate about what to eat is during the holidays. Whether we're celebrating Easter with a crawfish boil or the big holiday feasts that Thanksgiving and Christmas bring, my siblings and their families always come together to celebrate. We gather around the dining table remembering past times and catching up on what's new.

Julie and Joey

Linda's Oyster Patties

Yields 2 dozen

This Seventh Ward Creole favorite was served as a side dish for every Thanksgiving and Christmas on Columbus Street where my sister-in-law Linda grew up. I always look forward to having oyster patties every holiday. Create a new tradition within your own family and help keep this Seventh Ward Creole favorite alive.

Two dozen raw oysters
½ cup vegetable oil
½ cup all-purpose flour
2 bunches green onions, chopped
1 clove garlic, chopped
1 bunch flat parsley, chopped
½ tbsp. thyme
3 bay leaves
2 tbsp. granulated garlic
2 tbsp. granulated onion
Salt to taste
Pepper to taste
2 dozen large patty shells* baked, with any excess interior pastry scraped out.

Preheat oven to 350 degrees.

Strain oysters over a bowl, removing any oyster shells. Save oyster water.

In a large skillet, heat vegetable oil and add flour, stirring together to make light brown roux.

Add green onions to roux, sauté until slightly wilted. Add garlic, parsley, thyme, and bay leaves. Sauté until garlic is tender. Add oysters and cook for 5 minutes on a low fire.

Add oyster water until mixture is desired consistency. Add granulated garlic, granulated onion, salt, and pepper to taste. Simmer for 2-3 minutes.

Place one oyster in each patty shell and top with sauce. Replace lids on each patty shell. Bake stuffed patty shells at 350 degrees until bubbly and browned.

*Pepperidge Farms widely distributes vol-au-vent in grocery store's freezer cases. New Orleans bakeries often sell what we call patty shells locally.

Linda's Stuffed Mushrooms

Yields 20-24 mushrooms

Our holidays are all about food. When we gather, we begin eating while waiting for everyone to arrive. My sister-in-law Linda makes appetizers for us to munch on before everyone takes their seat at the table. Sometimes she serves oyster patties, but lately she has been making crabmeat stuffed mushrooms. These mushrooms have saved the day while we're waiting for my perennially late, brother Joey to arrive.

2 16-oz. containers medium white mushrooms, cleaned
8 tbsp. butter
½ bunch green onions, chopped
1 large green bell pepper, chopped
3 stalks celery, chopped
1 large onion, chopped
5 medium cloves garlic, finely minced
¼ cup Italian parsley, chopped
5 bay leaves
1 lb. claw crab meat
¾ cup Progresso Italian breadcrumbs
1 tbsp. granulated garlic
1 tbsp. granulated onion
Creole seasoning to taste

Remove mushroom stems from tops. Place aside the tops and finely chop the stems.

In a saucepan, melt butter. Add green onions, bell pepper, celery, onion, mushroom stems, garlic, and parsley. Cook together until wilted.

Add bay leaves, crabmeat, breadcrumbs, granulated garlic, and granulated onion. Cook for 7 minutes on medium heat, constantly stirring and regularly scraping the bottom of pot. Add Creole seasoning to taste.

Stuff mushroom caps with crabmeat dressing and bake at 375 degrees for 10 minutes.

*My brother-in-law Conway
and Momma*

Crawfish Boil Soup

Yields 6-8 servings

One of our annual traditions is a big, family crawfish boil on Good Friday. My brother Rivers is the king of boiled crawfish. Although typically, most people estimate 5 lbs. of crawfish per person along with lots of corn, potatoes, and smoked sausage. We always plan for 6-8 lbs. per person because then, we have tons of leftovers. Crawfish Boil Soup is one delicious way we use those leftovers. This soup is creamy, like a chowder, and full of flavor. It's also delicious, made with boiled shrimp or crabs.

4 tbsp. butter
¼ cup flour
1 medium onion, chopped
2 cups chicken broth
½ cup crawfish claws, divided in half
2-3 cups peeled crawfish
4-5 ears of corn, kernels cut from cob
12-15 potatoes, diced
1-2 lbs. smoked sausage, sliced into ½ inch rings
2 cups half and half
Salt to taste
Black pepper to taste
¼ cup chopped green onions and for garnish

Melt butter in saucepan. Whisk in flour, stirring constantly for 8-10 minutes. Add onions and cook until soft. Add chicken broth, whisking together until flour is dissolved. Add half of the crawfish claws and simmer for 30 minutes.

Add peeled crawfish, corn, potatoes, and sausage and simmer for 10 minutes. Reduce the heat and add half and half. Cook for another 5 minutes. Add salt and pepper to taste.

Serve with a sprinkle of chopped green onions and garnish with crawfish claws.

Crawfish Bisque

Yields 20 servings

Crawfish bisque is a special family treasure that we only serve once a year on Easter Sunday. Traditionally, we have a crawfish boil on Good Friday and keep the crawfish heads, tails, and some claws for our annual bisque. It is always served with potato salad using the eggs that were boiled and dyed for Easter baskets. To accomplish this time-consuming specialty, we make the bisque gravy one day, then wait until the next to make the stuffing and stuff the heads.

For Bisque Gravy

3 cups vegetable oil
3 cups flour
2 cups onion, chopped
2 cups chopped bell pepper,
2 cups celery, chopped
2 tbsp. garlic, minced
3 cups tomato sauce
1 12-oz. can tomato paste

4½ quarts seafood stock
1½ cups crawfish claws
4 lbs. Louisiana crawfish tails
2 cups green onions, chopped
1½ cup parsley, chopped
Creole seasoning and cayenne pepper to taste

In a 20-quart stock pot, heat oil over medium heat. Make a dark roux by adding flour and stirring constantly, being careful not to burn. Once the roux has reached a dark brown color, add onions, bell pepper, and celery. Sauté until vegetables are tender, about 5-8 minutes.

Add garlic and sauté for about 3 minutes. Add tomato sauce and paste to the vegetable mixture and mix well. Cook for five minutes, stirring constantly. Add stock and bring to a boil. Once it reaches a boil, reduce to low heat, and add the crawfish claws. Simmer together for about 30 minutes.

Add the crawfish tails and simmer over a low heat for 15-20 minutes. Add stuffed crawfish heads, green onions, and parsley and season to taste. Simmer for an additional 20 minutes. Serve over rice.

For Stuffing

3 lbs. crawfish tails
1 cup vegetable oil
1 cup all-purpose flour
4 cups onions, diced
2 cups celery, diced
2 cups green bell pepper, diced
½ cup green onion, diced
4 tbsp. garlic, minced
1 15-oz. can tomato sauce

5 bay leaves
1 cup Italian parsley, chopped
3 cups plain breadcrumbs
4 tbsp. melted butter
Creole Seasoning to taste
Cayenne pepper to taste
2 tbsp. garlic powder
2 tbsp. onion powder
120 cleaned crawfish heads

In a food processor, pulse crawfish tails until evenly chopped, set aside.

Heat oil in a large stock pot. Add flour, stirring constantly, cooking until a light brown.

Add onions, celery, bell pepper and cook until soft. Add green onion and garlic and cook for 3-5 minutes. Add tomato sauce and bay leaves and cook for 15 minutes. Add parsley, breadcrumbs, and butter, stirring well.

Add chopped crawfish tails and season to taste with Creole seasoning, cayenne pepper, garlic powder, and onion powder.

Stuff heads with crawfish stuffing and bake for 30 minutes at 350 degrees. Add stuffed heads to bisque.

Julie and Angela

Crab Au Gratin

Yields 6 servings

My sister Angela and I have very different cooking styles. She is a recipe cook, I'm not. Angela's food is always delicious but very different from mine. One of her specialties is crab au gratin. She makes this for special occasions and when entertaining. Sometimes it's served as a dip, other times as an entrée, but every time it's delicious.

4 tbsp. butter
2 tbsp. flour
3 green onions, chopped
¾ cup half and half
1½ cup grated sharp cheddar cheese
1 tsp. Creole seasoning
1 tsp. granulated garlic
½ tsp. cayenne pepper
1 lb. lump crabmeat

Melt butter in a saucepan on medium heat. Add flour, stirring carefully not to brown. Add green onions and cook for five minutes. Add half and half and stir until well blended. When the mixture starts to bubble, reduce heat to low and simmer, stirring constantly for 5 minutes. Mix in 1 cup of cheddar cheese and stir until completely blended. Add the Creole seasoning, granulated garlic, and cayenne pepper, stirring until combined.

Fold in the crabmeat, being careful not to break apart the lumps of crab. Pour mixture into a small baking dish and top with remaining cheddar cheese. Bake at 350 degrees for 15 minutes. Can be served with bread rounds.

Mrs. Blenda

Mrs. Blenda's Crab Casserole

Yields 12 servings

For many years, I managed senior apartments. I learned many things from my tenants. They shared advice like, "Make sure your husband eats peanuts to keep the lead in his pencil," or "Hoop earrings are man catchers." Another was, "If you walk wherever you need to go, you'll never walk into a doctor's office." I had many special tenants who affected my life. Many would bring me things to eat. It was their way of saying thank you for helping them with things. One of my tenants, Mrs. Blenda would always come to my office to chat. One day she brought me some of her crab casserole and it was amazing! She was kind enough to share the recipe with me and I use it for holidays and special meals. Mrs. Blenda insisted you have to use claw meat, because it has more flavor.

16 tbsp. butter
½ bunch Italian parsley, chopped
2 yellow onions, chopped
2 bunches green onion, chopped
½ large green bell pepper, chopped
1 stale loaf French bread
2 16-oz. containers claw crab meat
4 eggs, beaten
½ cup milk

Melt the butter in a large saucepan. Add parsley, yellow onions, green onions, and bell pepper. Sauté the vegetables until soft. Break the bread into small pieces and cook in the pan with the butter and vegetables for about 15 minutes. Add the crab meat and cook an additional 5 minutes. Remove from the heat.

Beat eggs with ½ cup of milk. Add to the crabmeat a little at a time, stirring so that eggs do not scramble. Place in a 9x13 inch casserole dish and bake for 20 minutes at 350 degrees.

Oyster Dressing

Yields 10 servings

Oyster dressing is a holiday favorite that we only make at Thanksgiving. This flavorful dressing was originally stuffed into the turkey and baked with all the juices of the bird, but now we just make it in a casserole to be served on the side of the roasted or fried turkey.

2 pints oysters
1 loaf stale French bread, cubed
1 lb. ground chuck
1 lb. Vaucresson Creole Hot
     Sausage, out of the casing
8 tbsp. butter
1½ onion, finely chopped
1 bell pepper, finely chopped
2 stalks celery, finely chopped

1 bunch green onions, chopped
5-6 cloves garlic, finely chopped
1 cup Italian parsley, chopped
1 cup chicken broth
1 bay leaf
½ tsp. dried thyme
⅛ tsp. dried sage
Creole Seasoning to taste
Black pepper to taste

Drain oysters, reserving oyster liquid. Chop one pint of the oysters coarsely and leave the remaining pint whole. Set oysters aside. Soak French bread in oyster liquid.

Brown ground chuck and the hot sausage in a heavy skillet. Drain off grease and set aside.

Add butter to skillet and melt over medium heat. Add onions, bell peppers, and celery and sauté until soft and translucent. Add green onions and garlic and cook for 3-5 minutes.

Mix in the ground chuck and hot sausage, combining thoroughly.

Stir in parsley and oysters, both whole and chopped. Cook until oysters' edges curl.

Wring out bread to remove excess liquid and make sure it's easy to break apart. Stir into oyster mixture and cook over a medium heat, adding small amounts of stock until desired consistency is reached. Add bay leaf, thyme, and sage. Season with Creole seasoning and black pepper to taste and pour into a greased 9x13 inch casserole dish.

Bake at 350 degrees for 20 minutes until browned and bubbly.

Ryan Carley and Hilary

Eggplant Dressing

Yields 8 servings

Eggplant dressing is something we only have on special occasions. One of my dearest friends, Ryan Carley loved my eggplant dressing. He would always ask me to make it whenever we were getting together. After a while, I gave him the recipe so he would stop working me to death and make it himself. Ryan passed away 10 years ago and how I wish I could make this dressing for him again. I think of him fondly whenever I cook it.

3 large or 4 medium eggplants
½ lb. Vaucresson Hot Sausage,
    out of the casing
½ lb. ground chuck
8 tbsp. butter
1 large onion, diced
1 large bell pepper, diced
3-4 cloves garlic, minced

1 lb. shrimp, peeled and deveined
¼ cup Italian parsley, finely chopped
1-2 cups chicken stock
1-2 cups breadcrumbs
1 tbsp. garlic powder
Creole Seasoning to taste
Black pepper to taste

Boil eggplants until soft but not mushy, about 10 minutes. Peel and remove any seeds.

Mash/purée the eggplant pulp and meat. Set aside. Thoroughly mix ground chuck with hot sausage. Set aside.

In a 5-quart deep skillet, brown the meat mixture. Drain off any excess grease and set aside.

In the same skillet, melt butter over medium heat. Add onions and bell pepper and sauté until soft. Add garlic and cook for 3 minutes. Return meat mixture to the pan, stirring to mix well. Add shrimp and cook until they just turn pink. Add eggplant, stirring well to combine. Add chopped parsley.

Add chicken stock, one half cup at a time until very moist. Stir in breadcrumbs until thickened and season to taste. Pour into a 5-quart casserole pan and sprinkle breadcrumbs on top. Bake for 35 minutes at 350 degrees until breadcrumbs are brown and toasted.

*May also add crabmeat, ham and/or smoked sausage.

Mirliton Dressing

Yields 10 servings

Every fall, my Aunt Alma would give us brown grocery bags filled with mirlitons from the vine that grew on her chain link fence. Mirliton vines were plentiful until our local vines died in Hurricane Katrina. I don't know many people with mirliton vines in New Orleans today, but imported ones known elsewhere as chayote squash are always available in the grocery stores. My mirliton casserole is a variation of my mother's traditional shrimp and ham stuffed mirliton. The addition of our famous Creole hot sausage brings the right level of spice and added flavor. Mom's individually stuffed mirlitons are lots of work, but when I make it as a casserole it's easy to prepare and it freezes well too.

¾ lb. of Vaucresson Creole Hot Sausage, out of the casing	1 lb. shrimp, peeled and deveined
6 mirlitons boiled until soft and cut in ½ lengthwise	1 bunch green onion, chopped
	¼ cup parsley, chopped
8 tbsp. butter	1 tsp. Lea & Perrins Worcestershire sauce
1 medium yellow onion, chopped	Creole seasoning to taste
¼ red bell pepper, chopped	Cayenne pepper to taste
¼ green bell pepper, chopped	1 egg, beaten
1 stalk of celery chopped	1½- 2 cups breadcrumbs
3-4 cloves garlic, finely chopped	8 oz. crabmeat (remove any shells)

Grease 9x13 inch baking pan and set aside.

In a 3-quart skillet, brown the sausage, then remove from the pan, draining on paper towel to eliminate any excess grease. Remove seeds from mirliton and discard. Scoop out the pulp, mash it, then reserve.

Melt butter in the same skillet, then add onions, bell peppers, and celery, cooking until soft. Add garlic and cook for 4 minutes. Add the shrimp to the seasonings and cook until just pink. Mix in the hot sausage and mashed mirliton pulp along with green onions and parsley.

Remove from the heat and season with Worcestershire sauce, Creole seasoning, and cayenne pepper, stirring to mix thoroughly. Quickly stir in the beaten egg so that it doesn't cook. Gradually add breadcrumbs, leaving some to top the dish with, until it reaches the desired thickness.

Add crabmeat, mixing carefully so the lumps of crab meat remain intact. Spoon into a greased casserole pan and top with remaining breadcrumbs. Bake at 350 degrees for about 20 minutes until browned and bubbly.

Green Bean and Artichoke Casserole

Yields 12 servings

My mother and I always battle about this recipe. She believes it's meant to be a holiday meal side dish. For her, there is too much added to the green beans for it to be considered just a vegetable. My nephews love it, so I overrule her and bring it to family gatherings anyway. This battle has continued for most of my adult life—with her insisting it's too much, and me making it anyway. My motto has always been more is more, so this recipe is a perfect vegetable dish for me.

3 15.5-oz. cans of French cut green beans, drained
2 14-oz. cans of artichoke hearts, drained and rinsed
1¾ cup plus ¼ cup Progresso Italian breadcrumbs (2 cups total)
1 cup grated parmesan cheese
1 cup shredded mozzarella cheese
2 tbsp. garlic powder
Creole seasoning to taste
Black pepper to taste
½ cup olive oil

Preheat oven to 375 degrees. In a large bowl, mix all ingredients together except for ¼ cup reserved breadcrumbs and olive oil.

Spoon into a 9x13 inch casserole pan. Sprinkle remaining ¼ cup of breadcrumbs evenly on top. Drizzle olive oil on top and cover with foil. Bake for 30 minutes covered.

Remove foil and bake for an additional 15-20 minutes until lightly browned on top.

Snap Beans with Potatoes and Sausage

Yields 8 servings

Every time we went to New Iberia, we came home with a bag of fresh vegetables. The vegetables were either given to us or we'd stop and purchase some from a farmer on the side of the road. Snap beans are the country name for green beans. No matter what you call them, they have always been one of my favorites to eat, but I hated the work that went into prepping them. It seemed like I was always the lucky one who had to snap the ends of the beans off. I would sit at the kitchen table for what seemed like hours breaking the ends until my little fingers hurt. In the end though, it was always so worth it. The beans, potatoes, and sausage always taste amazing!

1 lb. Vaucresson Creole Hot Sausage
1 lbs. red potatoes
4 tbsp. butter
1 medium onion, chopped
3 cloves garlic, chopped
2 lbs. snap beans, washed and ends snapped off
½ cup chicken broth
1 tbsp. Creole seasoning
1 tsp. granulated garlic
1 tsp. black pepper

In a saucepan, brown sausage. Remove from pan and place on a paper to drain any excess grease and set aside. Cut sausage into ¼-inch slices.

Wash and cut the potatoes into quarters and set aside. Heat the butter in a saucepan and sauté the onions until soft. Add the garlic and sauté for 3 minutes. Add the potatoes and cook for 5 minutes.

Add the sausage, green beans, and chicken broth. Cover and cook until beans are tender. Season with Creole seasoning, granulated garlic, and pepper.

Holiday Candied Yams

Yields 8-10 servings

Candied yams are so rich, sweet, and decadent, they're almost like eating dessert. Because they're so special, we only have them as a splurge on holidays.

6 medium sized yams, peeled and sliced
8 tbsp. butter
¼ cup white sugar
1 cup firmly packed dark brown sugar
1 tsp. ground cinnamon
¼ tsp. nutmeg
1 tbsp. vanilla extract

Place yams in a 9x13 baking dish. Melt butter and add the sugars, cinnamon, and nutmeg. Stir well and add vanilla extract. Pour butter mixture over the yams, evenly coating them. Cover with foil. Place small slits in the foil to vent.

Bake for 30 minutes. Then stir to rotate the yams, recover, and bake for an additional 25 minutes.

Julie and Hilary

CHAPTER TEN

Hot and Healing Soup

After my daughter Hilary was born, soup became my best friend. I was six months pregnant when we evacuated for Hurricane Katrina. I had to find new doctors and repeat all my prenatal tests. Since I lost my job after the storm, I had no private insurance. This presented many obstacles in finding quality healthcare. Our entire journey after the storm was not for the faint of heart. Having to start new relationships with new doctors while establishing ourselves in new surroundings presented many challenges.

Complications during and after the pregnancy made matters worse. My recovery was far from a normal one, and as my symptoms grew and became worse, I realized something else was terribly wrong. Feeling like I was dying inside, I desperately reached out to my longtime doctor, Jennifer Lapeyrolerie in New Orleans, hoping she was back at work. She was, and after my initial consultation I was rushed into surgery for what would be the first of five abdominal surgeries over the next seven months. There were many ICU stays, feeding tubes, and mental health struggles. At one point, I was terrified I wouldn't be around to raise my kids.

The biggest struggle was finding food my body would accept. The one tried and true sustenance my stomach would allow was soup. It gave me everything I needed and more. It was warm going down, soothing to my stomach, and was true comfort food. Knowing I could eat soup gave me confidence about my recovery. It gave me nutrients to get stronger and made me look at soup in a whole new way as I journeyed back to health.

My family has always enjoyed a steamy bowl of soup on a cold and dreary day. I remember preparing for an ice storm bearing down on New Orleans by making a big pot of beef and vegetable soup. The entire family was in pj's, enjoying our soup and watching a movie together when 5-year-old Hilary announced snow was coming in her room from the roof. Vance and I panicked, and ran into her room to find white dust sprinkled on the floor. We both dressed to go outside and investigate, fearing what we would find.

Freezing, we got the ladder and Vance climbed up on the icy roof to investigate, being careful not to slide off. It was so cold, but I stuck it out with him because we're a team—for better or for worse! After an extensive search, he couldn't locate the leak.

We told the kids that we couldn't find anything but would keep an eye on it and began to temporarily move Hilary out of her room. Neither of us could figure out where that fine white powder had come from. Hilary was squirming as she began to see the seriousness of the situation. She reached down and put her finger in the white dust and then in her mouth before confessing, "maybe it's just sugar." It seems she thought if there was a problem in her room, she might be able to go outside and play in the weather. We all needed a lot of delicious soup after that adventure.

Creamy Creole Chicken Sausage and Potato Soup

Yields 8 servings

This creamy, hearty soup is food for the soul. It's perfect no matter the weather. Rainy, sunny, chilly, or hot, when I crave some warm comfort food, this soup hits the spot!

1 lb. Vaucresson's Creole Chicken Sausage, out of the casing
4 tbsp. butter
¼ cup white flour
1 medium onion, finely chopped
1 stalk celery, finely chopped
3 cloves of garlic, finely chopped
4 cups chicken broth
1 lb. Russet potatoes, peeled and diced small
2 cups half and half
Creole Seasoning to taste
Pepper to taste

Brown the chicken sausage and put on a plate lined with a paper towel to drain any grease off. Set aside.

In a large soup pot, melt butter and whisk in flour. Cook for 5 minutes, stirring constantly. Add onion and celery and cook until soft, about 5 minutes. Add garlic and cook for about 3-4 minutes.

Whisk in the chicken broth, stirring until all the flour is dissolved. Add the potatoes and sausage and bring to a boil. Lower the fire and simmer for 15 minutes or until the potatoes are soft. Add the half and half, Creole seasoning, and pepper, and simmer for 5 minutes.

Can be garnished with crumbled bacon and or cheddar cheese.

Sweet Potato and Sausage Soup

Yields 6 servings

When my daughter Hilary was in 4th grade, she and her friends started the "I Hate Sweet Potatoes" club. She was the vice president and took her role very seriously. They would meet to discuss how much they hated sweet potatoes. I thought this was the most ridiculous thing and still continued to cook sweet potatoes. I thought that I had converted Hilary with this soup, but she stood strong in her oath. Although she would never say it, I think secretly, she really likes sweet potatoes. I'm glad she's still an active club member though, because that means more sweet potatoes for me!

1 lb. Vaucresson's Creole Hot Sausage, out of the casing
8 tbsp. butter
2 lbs. sweet potatoes, peeled and diced
2 large carrots, peeled and chopped
2 celery stalks, chopped
1 large onion, chopped
3 cloves garlic, minced
6 cups chicken stock
2 cups half and half
Creole seasoning to taste
Cayenne pepper to taste

Brown sausage and drain excess grease, set aside. Reserve 6 tsps. for garnish.

Melt butter in a large stock pot and sauté sweet potatoes until soft, about 8 minutes. Add carrots, celery, and onion and cook until translucent. Add garlic and cook for 3 minutes. Add the chicken stock and simmer 10 minutes or until the sweet potatoes are thoroughly cooked.

Purée the soup with an immersion blender or food processor until smooth. Return to stockpot and add sausage and half and half and cook on low for 5 minutes. Do not allow to boil.

Serve with 1 tsp. crumbled sausage on top of each bowl and season to taste.

Linda's Corn and Crab Soup

Yields 8 servings

My sister-in-law Linda makes a wonderful corn and crab soup. She always serves it for special occasions when we begin the meal with a soup or gumbo. Corn and crab soup is a favorite with our whole family. If it's on the menu when we're out for dinner, Vance and VJ always order it. This rich, delicate soup always makes for a memorable meal.

8 tbsp. butter
¼ cup all-purpose flour
1 large yellow onion, chopped
3 stalks celery, chopped
1 large green bell pepper, chopped
1 bunch green onion, chopped
1 tbsp. garlic, finely chopped
1 tbsp. Italian parsley, chopped
5 bay leaves
1 14.75-oz. can cream style corn
1 10-oz. bag frozen yellow corn, thawed
3 cups half and half
1 cup shrimp stock
1 lb. lump crabmeat
Creole seasoning to taste
Cayenne pepper to taste
1 tsp. granulated garlic
1 tsp. granulated onion
1 pinch of thyme

Melt butter in a large stock pot. Whisk in flour and cook until it's a very light brown color, about 3-5 minutes. Add onion, celery, bell pepper, green onion, garlic, and parsley. Sauté together until wilted.

Add bay leaves, cream style corn, and frozen yellow corn. Simmer together for 7 minutes. Add half and half and shrimp stock and continue simmering on a low fire for four minutes, then carefully fold in crab meat, keeping lumps intact. Add Creole seasoning, cayenne pepper, granulated garlic, granulated onion, and thyme. Cook over a low heat for 3 minutes, being careful not to boil which will curdle the half and half.

Linda's Okra Gumbo

Yields 15-20 servings

Okra gumbo is a family favorite. My mother would buy bushels of okra during the summer. It was a tedious task to clean, cut, and precook all of it. We would spend hours cutting, cooking, and bagging the okra to freeze for future use. My sister-in-law Linda is the gumbo queen and makes the best gumbo in our family. Her okra gumbo is to die for and I'm fortunate to have her recipe.

4 lbs. okra, cut into ¼ inch slices
¼ cup olive oil
½ cup vegetable oil
½ cup flour
2 large yellow onions, chopped
2 large bell peppers, chopped
4 stalks celery, chopped
1 tbsp. parsley, chopped
2 tbsp. garlic, chopped
½ cup crushed tomatoes
2 lbs. smoked sausage, sliced in
    1-inch pieces

2 lbs. diced ham
64 oz. unsalted chicken broth
7 bay leaves
Creole seasoning to taste
Black pepper to taste
2 tbsp. granulated garlic
2 tbsp. granulated onion
2 lbs. shrimp, peeled and deveined
6 blue crabs, cleaned

Preheat oven to 350 degrees.

Spread okra on a large baking pan and sprinkle with olive oil.

Bake at 350 degrees, stirring every 5 minutes until slime is gone, about 15 minutes in total.

In a large gumbo pot, heat vegetable oil on a low fire. Whisk in flour to make a roux. Cook, stirring continuously for about 20 minutes until the roux reaches a rich, medium brown color. Add onions, bell pepper, celery, parsley, and chopped garlic and sauté until soft.

Add crushed tomatoes, okra, smoked sausage, and ham. Cook over medium to low heat for 10 minutes. Add chicken broth, bay leaves, Creole seasoning, black pepper, granulated garlic, and granulated onion. Simmer over a medium to low fire for 25 minutes. Add shrimp and crabs and cook for an additional 15 minutes. Serve over rice.

Renee Lapeyrolerie and her heirloom mirliton

Mirliton Soup

Yields 8 servings

One of my dearest friends, Renee Lapeyrolerie, is a mirliton enthusiast. She even has her own mirliton variety. The Renee Lapeyrolerie heirloom mirliton is registered and named specially for her. Renee grows the most beautiful mirlitons around. It is such a special treat when she gifts me with some because they taste so much better straight off the vine.

4 tbsp. butter
1 medium onion, chopped
2 cloves garlic, minced
1 cup diced ham
1 lb. shrimp, peeled and deveined
6 mirlitons, boiled, peeled, and pureed
1 pint claw crabmeat
3 cups chicken broth
½ cup half and half
1 tbsp. Creole seasoning
1 tsp. granulated garlic
1 tsp. granulated onion
Cayenne pepper to taste

Melt butter in a large stock pot over medium heat. Add onions and sauté until soft and translucent. Add garlic and cook for 3 minutes. Add the ham and shrimp and cook until the shrimp turn pink.

Stir in the pureed mirliton and mix well. Add the crabmeat, chicken broth, and half and half. Add Creole seasoning, granulated garlic, and granulated onion, mixing well. Season to taste with cayenne pepper. Simmer on low for 5 minutes and serve.

VJ and Julie

CHAPTER ELEVEN

My Family's Creole Favorites

For years I heard stories about a traditional Creole man, but I never understood what that meant, although now I know my husband and my son are both just that. I remember being in the hair salon with my mom as a little girl, hearing ladies talk about how there were certain things their Creole husbands expected of them. There were plenty of jokes about being married to a Creole man.

One thing that stood out to me was their husband's expectations at dinner. It seemed Creole men were served their dinner first and always got the best and biggest piece of meat. Most importantly, the wives always made sure to wear lipstick. First thing in the morning when they got up to make breakfast, they had to at least put on lipstick, if not full makeup. I vowed to never let a man put any expectations or demands like that on me.

Fast forward to February 2006. We were living in a trailer on family land in New Iberia, Louisiana, after losing our home and business in Hurricane Katrina. My daughter Hilary was 2 months old and we were just settling into a routine. VJ, my eldest, was at day care with his cousins to give him some sense of normalcy.

He loved it there, and things were going well until my five-year-old son began coming home to request things "the lady in the cafeteria cooked." He would ask me, "Mom, can you cook big, hot, juicy meatballs with spaghetti like Ms. Yvella cooks? Mom, can you buy this delicious green melon like Ms. Yvella? Mom, Ms. Yvella makes the crispy fried catfish every Friday."

The list went on and I worked hard to accommodate. He came home one day and while pointing at the clock on the microwave he declared, "Mom, when the clock is on the six, that's when I want my dinner." He was very emphatic when he told me that he expected to eat "on the six" while still pointing at the clock. "Mom, that is the best time for dinner, ok? I want my food on the table when the clock is on the six." I had already started cooking

VJ in his favorite place

all the things he requested, and now he wanted me to come home and make sure dinner was always ready "on the six."

Even now that VJ is in college, he often calls home close to six o'clock to see what we're eating for dinner while he's walking to the dining hall. Even after all this time, we still try to have dinner "on the six."

After swearing I'd never jump through hoops for a demanding Creole man, it seems I not only married one, I've raised one too!

VJ's Spicy Meatloaf

Yields 8 servings

I never thought I would cater to a man until I had my son VJ. When he about 5 years old he told me that he liked to eat his dinner, "When the clock is on the 6." He insisted that was the perfect dinner time. From that day forward, I would rush home and try to have dinner on the table, "on the 6." Even as a grown man, he looks for his dinner "on the 6," and I'm the type of mom to comply.

1 lb. ground sirloin
1 lb. Vaucresson's Creole hot sausage, out of the casing
1 cup breadcrumbs
1 tbsp. Lea & Perrins Worcestershire sauce
1 large egg
1 tsp. garlic powder
1 tsp. onion powder
Salt to taste
Black pepper to taste

Preheat oven to 350 degrees. In a large bowl, mix together all ingredients well. Put into a loaf pan.

Bake for 50 minutes covered, then broil for an additional 5-10 minutes until well browned.

Let meatloaf rest for 5 minutes before serving. Serve meatloaf slices with garlic mashed potatoes and brown gravy.

Brown Gravy

Yields 6 servings

6 tbsp. vegetable oil
6 tbsp. all-purpose flour
3 cups beef broth
1 tsp. beef bouillon
1 tsp. Lea & Perrins Worcestershire sauce
1 tsp. granulated garlic
2 tsps. Creole seasoning

Heat oil and add flour. Cook over medium heat, stirring constantly for 8-10 minutes, allowing flour to brown to a deep rich color. Add the beef broth, bouillon, Worcestershire sauce, and spices. Let the gravy simmer on a low fire. If you have any meat drippings, add for more flavor.

Garlic Mashed Potatoes

Yields 6-8 servings

3 lbs. russet potatoes, washed and peeled
1 tsp. salt
8 tbsp. butter
4 cloves garlic, finely minced
¾ cup heavy whipping cream
1 tsp. Creole seasoning
1 tsp. black pepper
1 cup chicken broth

Cut potatoes into quarters and add them to a pot of salted water. Boil until potatoes are soft. Drain the potatoes and leave them in the pot.

While potatoes are boiling, melt the butter in a small saucepan and add the garlic. Cook for 3 minutes on a low fire, stirring constantly. Add cream, Creole seasoning, and black pepper and let simmer on low for 5 minutes.

Mash the potatoes and then pour the cream mixture over them. Thoroughly mix the cream and potatoes together. If the potatoes are too stiff, gradually add chicken broth to get to the desired consistency.

Broccoli and Cauliflower Casserole

Yields 10 servings

My son VJ loves this casserole. I tasted something similar at a friend's house, but before I had finished the meal, I was thinking about how I would cook this at home and make it better. This is something I'm always doing. I'll eat something in a restaurant, then go home and recreate the dish, making it my own. Once I got this recipe down, I remember cooking this for a teacher appreciation lunch. VJ was horrified that I would be making broccoli and cauliflower. He was so embarrassed that I would actually send vegetables for the special lunch. But he came home that day and said that several teachers wanted the recipe. He was so intrigued that he wanted to try it himself. When he tasted it, his face lit up and he told me it was the best veggies he had ever had. Since then, it is regularly part of the Vaucresson family dinner rotation.

4 tbsp. butter, divided in two
½ cup Progresso Herb & Garlic breadcrumbs
¼ cup grated Parmesan cheese
2 tbsp. flour
1 medium onion, chopped
Creole seasoning to taste
Cayenne pepper to taste
1 tbsp. granulated garlic
1¼ cup half and half
4 oz. Philadelphia cream cheese, room temperature
1 lb. bag of frozen broccoli florets, thawed
1 lb. bag of frozen cauliflower florets, thawed

Melt 2 tbsp. of butter. In a bowl, mix breadcrumbs with 2 tbsp. of Parmesan cheese and the melted butter, then set aside.

In a large skillet, melt the remaining 2 tbsp. of butter and add the flour, stirring constantly for 5 minutes, being careful it doesn't brown. Add the onions and cook until translucent. Season the onions and flour with Creole seasoning, cayenne pepper, and granulated garlic. Add the half and half and stir until thickened.

Add the Philadelphia cream cheese and remaining Parmesan cheese, stirring until cream cheese is completely melted. Add the broccoli and cauliflower and stir until completely coated.

Pour mixture into a 9x13 baking dish and top with the bread crumb mixture. Bake at 350 degrees for 45 minutes or until the top is a golden brown.

Shrimp, Bacon, and Hot Sausage Quiche

Yields 8 slices

I have always loved quiche. It's a delicately delicious food that can be served for breakfast, lunch, or dinner. When I worked at the Housing Authority of New Orleans, there was a lunch spot near my office where I loved to get a slice of quiche with a side salad and a glass of hibiscus tea. It was one of my favorite lunches and where my love of quiche began.

1 9-inch pie crust
½ lb. Vaucresson's Creole Hot Sausage, out of the casing
4 slices thick cut bacon
1 lb. shrimp, peeled and deveined
3-4 cloves garlic, finely chopped
4 green onions, chopped
1 cup half and half
4 large eggs
½ tsp. Creole seasoning
½ cup shredded Swiss cheese
½ cup shredded cheddar cheese

Preheat oven to 350 degrees. Bake pie crust for about 10 minutes. Let cool.

In a heavy skillet, brown sausage, then drain well on paper towel and reserve. To the same pan, add bacon, frying until crispy. Cool on paper towel and then crumble into pieces. Set aside 2 tbsp. of crumbled bacon for garnish. Add shrimp and garlic to the bacon grease and cook until shrimp turn pink.

Set aside 2 tbsp. of green onion for garnish. In a bowl, whisk together half and half, eggs, green onions, and Creole seasoning. Put the shrimp, sausage, and bacon in the pie crust and top with egg and milk mixture.

Bake at 350 degrees on the lower oven rack for 35-40 minutes, leaving the center slightly jiggly.

Garnish the top with reserved green onions and bacon.

Creole Lasagna

Serves 8

Vaucresson's Italian Sausage makes any lasagna Creole. The whole family can't wait till the bubbling pan of lasagna comes out of the oven. Between the convenience of the Italian sausage, the pre-made pasta sauce and the no boil lasagna noodles, I can even pull this off on occasional weeknights.

2 lbs. Vaucresson's Italian Sausage, out of the casing
1 onion, chopped
3 stalks celery, chopped
1 green bell pepper, chopped
3 cloves garlic, chopped
1 quart jar pasta sauce
1 tsp. dried basil
½ tsp. dried oregano
1 tsp. Creole seasoning
½ tsp. sugar
1 cup ricotta cheese
4 tbsp. Italian parsley, chopped
4 tbsp. heavy cream
1 9-oz. box no-boil lasagna noodles
1½ cups grated mozzarella cheese, divided in thirds
1 cup Romano cheese, divided in thirds

Brown sausage in a heavy, 5-quart saucepot. Add onion, celery, bell pepper, and garlic. Sauté over a medium heat until soft. Add pasta sauce, basil, oregano, Creole seasoning, and sugar to the saucepot. Simmer together for 30 minutes.

Combine the ricotta cheese with the parsley and cream. Divide in half. Spread ¼ cup of meat sauce on the bottom of a 9x13 baking pan. Add a layer of lasagna noodles, topped with meat sauce, ricotta, mozzarella and Romano cheeses. Add a second layer of lasagna noodles and repeat ricotta, mozzarella and Romano cheese. Add a final layer of lasagna noodles, top with the last of the meat sauce and finish with mozzarella and Romano cheese. Add ½ cup water for every five no-boil noodles used. Cover pan tightly with aluminum foil.

Bake in a preheated 350-degree oven for 45 minutes. Remove the foil and bake for an additional 15 minutes until browned. Remove from oven and let rest for 10 minutes before serving.

Creole Italian Sausage and Peppers

Yields 6-8 servings

This dinner is so fast and easy, it's on the table in no time.

2 lbs. Creole Italian sausage
1 red bell pepper, sliced
1 green bell pepper, sliced
1 large onion, sliced
1 quart jar pasta sauce
2 cloves garlic, chopped
1 tsp. Creole seasoning
1 lb. spaghetti, cooked al dente
¼ cup Parmesan cheese

Brown sausages in a 3-quart skillet. Remove and set aside.

Add peppers and onions to the skillet and sauté together until they begin to soften. Return sausage to the pan and add pasta sauce, garlic and Creole seaoning. Simmer together for 15-20 minutes.

Serve sausages whole or sliced on top of spaghetti with Parmesan cheese sprinkled on top.

CHAPTER TWELVE

Making Up Mustards

The 2019 festival season was a turning point in my career. As I was doing the books from the festivals, I noticed that we were buying an extremely large amount of mustard. We buy a lot of condiments, but mustard was the real front runner.

I'm always coming up with ideas, but this one was different. I explained it to Vance, showing him the numbers and what we were spending on condiments, particularly mustard. Then, I suggested to him that we make our own mustard and condiment line. That way we could have mustards and sauces that perfectly pair with our sausage but could be stand-alone products as well. Vance said he thought it was a great idea and that he would support me, but I never heard him mention it again.

On the other hand, I was super excited about this venture. I started reading all about mustard and condiments. I hired a recipe developer to help me develop baseline recipes. Once she turned them over to me, I adjusted and tweaked the flavors to get them exactly where I wanted them.

The big joke in my house was that I was tying up all the space in our refrigerator with mustard. Everybody viewed it as my hobby, but it was a lot more than a hobby for me. I gave samples to everyone I could find. I did much research on other brands and competitors before I sought out three different co-packers to produce the mustard, but for various reasons none of them worked out. Finally, all the stars lined up and I found a co-packer to manufacture the mustard. I received a small business loan to make it happen.

I had a vision and a dream, and I knew the only one who could make it happen was me. Once again, I had to "think outside the casing" to bring my dream to reality. If I was going to sell this, I had to put myself out there and tell the world how special my mustards were while showing them the magic they could do with our sausage. From this, the Creole Sausage Queen was born.

The Creole Sausage Queen is an alter ego that is super confident, extraverted, and witty. She totally has it all together—unlike me. She is able to do cooking segments on live TV, make presentations in front of large groups, and is super confident in everything she does. She is creative and a really good cook. She doesn't doubt herself. Sometimes I think the Creole Sausage Queen is the total opposite of me.

For many years, I was content to remain in the background and be whatever the family and business needed. But when I got the call to showcase my recipes on the news, it changed my whole outlook on my life. What's there to be nervous about? The Creole Sausage Queen is a superhero in the house, and you can be too. I am so much more than a wife, mother, sister, and friend. I am talented, I have a voice, and I can do anything when I work hard.

It still surprises me when I am shopping in TJ Maxx or Walmart and someone comes up and asks if I am the Sausage Queen or, when they say they saw me on Fox 8 and my recipe looked delicious. I am so humbled by the support. I have a wonderful circle of friends and have expanded it to include other female entrepreneurs.

In the kitchen with Momma

If I ever start to get cocky, my family will knock me right back in place. Several years ago, I told my daughter Hilary that I was going to volunteer to speak at her school for career day. She quickly asked, "So what's your career?" I told her that I would speak as an entrepreneur, Creole cook, on air personality, mustard mogul, restaurateur, and author. Hilary said, "Okay mom, let's not get ahead of ourselves."

A year later she came back to me and told me how proud she is of me, how amazing it's been for her to watch me build a brand separate from her dad's. This is why I do what I do. I do it because I love it, it's a passion of mine, and my daughter is watching.

Creole Coleslaw

Yields 6-8 servings

I love coleslaw. It's my favorite side with barbeque and baked beans and the perfect dressing on my pulled pork sandwiches. Adding our Creole Green Onion Sauce to the coleslaw gives a flavorful twist to whatever it's served with.

1 14-oz. bag of shredded coleslaw mix
½ cup mayonnaise
¼ cup Vaucresson's Creole Green Onion Sauce
1 tbsp. white sugar
¼ tsp. black pepper

Combine all the ingredients in a large mixing bowl. Refrigerate for an hour before serving.

Creole Mustard Honey Wings

Yields 5 servings

This Creole mustard and honey combination is the perfect way to surprise a crowd with a platter of spicy, delicious wings.

3-4 lbs. chicken wings (approximately 20 drums and flats)
1 tbsp. Creole seasoning
1 tbsp. black pepper
1 tbsp. garlic powder
½ tsp. paprika
¾ cup honey
¾ cup Vaucresson's Creole Mustard
1 tbsp. red pepper flakes

Preheat oven to 400 degrees.

In a large bowl, mix Creole seasoning, black pepper, garlic powder, and paprika. Add chicken pieces and toss in dry mixture until coated.

Place chicken on a foil lined pan and bake for 40 minutes.

In a small saucepan combine honey, Vaucresson's Creole Mustard, and red pepper flakes. Heat over a medium to low fire stirring occasionally.

Remove the wings from the oven and toss wings in honey mustard mixture. Return wings to baking pan and bake for an additional ten minutes at 400 degrees

Turn on broiler and broil wings on high for 3-5 minutes, watching closely not to burn.

Remove wings from the oven and cool slightly before serving.

Creole Smoked Ribs

Yields 6 servings

Vance is a beast on the grill. It's his thing. If we go to a cookout, he will find his way to the grill and take over. He has perfected his craft and Vance's ribs are unmatched.

1 slab baby back ribs
1 tsp. salt
1 tsp. pepper
1 tsp. garlic powder
½ cup Vaucresson's Creole Mustard
Barbeque sauce (optional)

Remove the membrane from the slab of ribs. Season the ribs with salt, pepper, and garlic powder on both sides of the stalks. Liberally coat the ribs on both sides with mustard.

Cook in 225-degree smoker for 3 hours. If using barbeque sauce, coat ribs for the last 30 minutes of cooking.

Creole Barbeque Sauce

Yields 1/4 cup

Grilling is a big thing in my house. Vance loves the grill and VJ is starting to follow in his footsteps. The two of them have different ideas about how to season their ribs, but one thing they do agree on is that adding our mustard makes a world of difference in the flavor.

4 tbsp. butter
1 medium yellow onion, chopped
3 cloves garlic, finely minced
½ cup ketchup
¼ cup water

2 tbsp. vinegar
1 tbsp. brown sugar
1 tsp. Creole seasoning
1 tbsp. Vaucresson's Creole Mustard
½ tsp. cayenne pepper

In a large saucepan, melt butter. Add onions and garlic and sauté until tender. Mix in the remaining ingredients and bring to a boil. Remove from heat and cool before using.

Apple Jelly and Mustard Glazed Pork Loin

Yields 8 servings

When we returned home after Hurricane Ida, we had extreme evacuation fatigue. We had lost all the food in our refrigerator and freezer due to the power outages, and supplies in the grocery stores were limited. The only thing I could find to make a meal with was a pork loin, a bag of potatoes, and some canned vegetables. Nobody wanted pork loin, but it was all we had, so they were stuck. I knew I had to somehow make this meal special. I started playing with the flavors, but once I added our Creole mustard, I knew I'd knocked it out the park.

1 3-lb. pork tenderloin
2 tbsp. Creole seasoning
2 tbsp. garlic powder
1 tsp. black pepper
1 tbsp. cooking oil
¼ cup Vaucresson's Creole Mustard
½ cup apple jelly
¼ cup brown sugar
½ tsp. cayenne pepper

Preheat oven to 425 degrees.

Generously coat the tenderloin on all sides with Creole seasoning, garlic powder, and pepper.

Heat oil in a heavy skillet and brown the pork loin on all sides.

Place the pork loin in a covered roasting pan and bake approximately 8 minutes per lb. Remove from oven and coat with mustard. Reduce oven to 375 degrees.

In a saucepan, heat Creole mustard, apple jelly, brown sugar, and cayenne pepper until sugar dissolves and mixture begins to bubble, about 5 minutes. Coat pork loin with glaze.

Cover and bake for 15-20 minutes. Let rest 8-10 minutes before serving.

CHAPTER THIRTEEN

Sweet Dreams

By the time you reach this chapter, you've probably guessed our whole family has a serious sweet tooth. With our crowd, no matter how filling dinner might be, I'd better have a plan for dessert.

We all have our favorites, and there are certain must have cakes for birthday celebrations. Since my brothers were little boys, Rivers insisted on pineapple upside down cake for his birthday and Joey comes looking for his carrot cake. When either of those cakes appear on other occasions, their grins spread from ear to ear.

Vance's mom, Geraldine loved Heavenly Hash, a favorite New Orleans Easter candy from Elmer's Chocolates. Once we mastered Heavenly Hash cake, Geraldine could indulge in her favorite flavors all year round. Even in summer, our family has dessert traditions thanks to River's wife, Linda's banana split cake.

But in Julie V's busy world, sometimes there's just no time for elaborate preparations, especially on weeknights. That's when my college roommate, Rosalyn's peach cobbler comes in handy and thank goodness, my quick apple crumble is exactly that—quick!

Needless to say, there's always ice cream in our freezer for à la mode. Or on nights when there might not be dessert planned, a bowl of ice cream keeps my troops happy.

Dessert at the Vaucresson house always guarantees sweet dreams!

Momma and Joey

Quick Apple Crumble Dessert

Yields 8 servings

I have tried to keep up my mama's tradition of dessert with Sunday dinner. Sometimes when I'm adventurous, I'll even make dessert during the week. Weekday desserts need to be quick and easy. This one is not only quick and easy, its real comfort food, especially when served with vanilla ice cream.

1 21-oz. can apple pie filling
1 tsp. ground cinnamon
½ tsp. nutmeg
8 tbsp. butter
1 15.25-oz. box yellow cake mix

Preheat the oven to 350 degrees.

Spread the pie filling in a 9x12 baking dish. Evenly sprinkle the cinnamon and nutmeg over the pie filling. Mix the cake mix with the butter until crumbly. Sprinkle over the pie filling.

Bake at 350 degrees until the top is brown, and the pie filling is bubbling. Serve with whipped topping or vanilla ice cream. Walnuts can be added to the crumble topping.

Creole Bread Pudding

Yields 8 servings

We had dessert at every Sunday dinner. Sometimes it was a cake, sometimes a pie, but many times it was bread pudding. My mother loved French bread, but it became stale so quickly, she hated to see it go to waste. If she didn't make bread pudding, she would make her own breadcrumbs. This recipe is a combination of my mother's and my dear cousin Tanya Boutte's recipes. I took the best from both! When mom made bread pudding, she would make half the pan with raisins and half without. I was team "no raisins" so this recipe doesn't have any, but you can always add them.

8 tbsp. butter
1½ cup whole milk
1 14-oz. can condensed milk
1 12-oz. can evaporated milk
4 eggs, beaten
1 tsp. vanilla extract
2 tsp. cinnamon
1 tsp. nutmeg
1 cup white sugar
1 cup brown sugar
3 cups stale French bread, cut into ½ inch cubes

Melt butter in the bottom of a 9x12-inch baking pan, distributing evenly. Combine fresh, condensed, and evaporated milks, eggs, vanilla extract, cinnamon, nutmeg, and sugars in a large bowl and mix well.

Pour melted butter from the pan into the bowl, leaving a coating on the bottom of the pan. Add the bread cubes to the milk mixture and soak for 2-4 hours. Pour the bread and milk mixture into butter coated pan and bake at 350 degrees for 45 minutes.

Momma's bread pudding is so delicious, no topping is needed!

Rosalyn's Peach Cobbler

Yields 8 servings

Rosalyn Thompson and I met freshman year in the dorm. We were at the University of Southwestern Louisiana. After our first year, we both transferred to other colleges. I went to Xavier University in New Orleans and she went to Texas Southern. But our one year together was special. We became quick friends and have remained close for more than thirty-five years. When Roz learned that I was working on a cookbook, my always supportive friend said, "I have some delicious recipes that I want to share." These party recipes are from Roz's hit parade and people are always asking her to share them. Although we don't live in the same city, our connection is strong and our bond unbreakable. I thank her for both these delicious recipes and for her friendship.

8 tbsp. butter
1 cup flour
1 cup sugar
1 cup milk
2 tsps. baking powder
Pinch salt
Pinch cinnamon, optional
2 15-oz. cans of peaches

Preheat oven to 350 degrees. In the warming oven, melt the butter in a 9x9-inch pan.

In a medium bowl, mix flour, sugar, milk, baking powder, and salt thoroughly. Once the butter is melted, remove the pan from the oven and pour the batter mixture over it. Spoon the peaches with the juice on top of the batter. Do not mix.

Bake at 350 degrees for 30-35 minutes and serve warm.

Buttermilk Pie

Yields 8 servings

This pie is a perfect dessert for Sunday dinner. I fell in love with it after I first tasted it at a friend's house and was determined to recreate this simply delicious pie. After numerous attempts, I not only replicated it, but mine is better!

1 cup buttermilk
3 eggs
1 tsp. vanilla
8 tbsp. butter, softened
Pinch of nutmeg
Pinch of cinnamon
2 cups white sugar
2 tsps. flour
1 9-inch premade pie crust

Preheat oven to 350 degrees.

Mix all ingredients together then pour into a 9-inch pie crust. Bake at 350 degrees for 45-50 minutes until pie is fully set. Cool before slicing.

Rivers and his favorite cake

Pineapple Upside Down Cake

Yields 12 servings

For our birthdays, my mom always allowed us to pick our favorite meal and cake for dinner. My older brother Rivers, affectionately known as Bud, always wanted pineapple upside down cake. I can't remember his birthday meal because he never really had a favorite dish. Bud loved everything! My mother had a special pan that she used to bake this cake. It seemed like she had special pots and pans for everything she cooked, and she was religious about using them. Unfortunately, she lost all of those pots and pans to Hurricane Katrina. But Katrina didn't get the recipes or the memories.

4 tbsp. butter
1 cup firmly packed light brown sugar
1 20-oz. can pineapple slices, drained, reserve juice
1 6-oz. jar maraschino cherries, drained and stems removed
1 15.25-oz. box yellow cake mix

Preheat oven to 350 degrees. Melt butter in a 12-inch skillet in the oven. Pour the brown sugar evenly over the butter. Arrange the pineapple slices on the brown sugar and place a cherry in the center of each one. Place additional cherries around the pineapple slices. Press pineapples and cherries into the brown sugar.

Prepare the cake mix according to the instructions, substituting 1 cup of plain water with the reserved pineapple juice and water to equal 1 cup total. Pour the batter on top of the pineapples and cherries.

Bake 40 minutes or until a toothpick comes out clean. Use a knife to loosen the cake from the pan. Put a serving platter on top of the cake pan and then turn cake over, letting the pan sit on top of the cake so all the brown sugar can coat the top of the cake. Let cake cool before serving.

Carrot Cake

Yields 8 servings

Carrot cake was my brother Joey's favorite. He would request it every year for his birthday. Joey would try to hide the cake to make sure there was more for him. He felt since it was made for his birthday, he was entitled to more than his fair share. My mother used to make it with an orange glaze, now I make it with a cream cheese frosting. Either way, Joey loves it.

2 cups of sugar
1½ cups vegetable oil
4 eggs
2 cups sifted flour
2 tsp. cinnamon
2 tsp. baking soda
2 tsp. baking powder
1 tsp. salt
3 cups grated carrots
1 cup chopped pecans, reserve ½ cup for topping

Preheat oven to 325 degrees.

Beat sugar and oil until blended. Add eggs one at a time, beating after each addition. Sift dry ingredients into sugar and oil mixture. Add carrots and pecans and mix well. Pour batter into 3 greased 9-inch cake pans. Bake at 325 degrees for 45 minutes. Cool, then frost with cream cheese icing.

Sprinkle reserved ½ cup chopped pecans on cake top to decorate.

Cream Cheese Frosting

1 lb. box powdered sugar
4 tbsp. butter
1 8-oz. package Philadelphia cream cheese
2 tsp. of vanilla

Combine all the ingredients and beat until mixture is spreading consistently. It will be stiff at first but soften after being well mixed.

Banana Split Cake

Yields 12 servings

When VJ and Hilary were growing up, Linda, my brother Rivers' wife always made this cake when we came to their house to swim. It was part of our family's summer routine—swimming, grilling, ice cream, and banana split cake. It was a delicious tradition, and all the kids loved it. It brings back warm memories of those summers past every time I have this cake.

2 cups graham cracker crumbs
1 cup white sugar
8 tbsp. melted butter
1 8-oz. package Philadelphia cream cheese
1½ cup powdered sugar
4 ripe bananas, sliced
1 cup strawberries, chopped
1 20-oz. can crushed pineapple, drained
1 8-oz. container Cool Whip
½ cup chocolate syrup
½ cup chopped peanuts

Combine the graham cracker crumbs, sugar, and butter. Firmly press into the bottom of a 9x13-inch baking dish and refrigerate until set, approximately 30 minutes.

Using an electric hand mixer, beat the cream cheese and powdered sugar on medium speed until well blended. Spread the cream cheese mixture over the graham cracker crust. Arrange the bananas, strawberries, and pineapple on top of the cream cheese mixture. Cover with Cool Whip and drizzle with chocolate syrup. Sprinkle the peanuts on top and refrigerate for 2 hours. Serve cold.

7 Up Cake

Yields 10 servings

Sometimes the best foods are simple and uncomplicated. 7 Up cake definitely fits that description. Buttery with the right amount of sweetness, this cake is perfect for everything from Sunday dinner to holiday meals.

3 cups sugar
2 cups butter, softened
5 eggs
3 cups cake flour
1 tsp. almond extract
2 tsps. vanilla extract
¾ cup 7 Up

Preheat oven to 350 degrees.

Grease a Bundt pan and set aside. Using a handheld or stand mixer, cream together sugar, butter, and eggs. With the mixer running, add flour, one cup at a time. Add almond and vanilla extracts and 7 Up, mixing well. Batter should be thick but smooth.

Pour into a greased Bundt pan. Bake for an hour at 350 degrees until an inserted toothpick comes out cleanly. Allow to cool before removing from Bundt pan.

Glaze with powdered sugar glaze.

Easy Powdered Sugar Glaze

2 cups powdered sugar
3-4 tbsp. whole milk
1 tsp. almond extract

In a medium mixing bowl, whisk together powdered sugar, 3 tbsp. milk, and almond extract. Whisk until the desired consistency, adding more milk if necessary. Pour over the cooled cake and serve.

Geraldine Dave Vaucresson

Heavenly Hash Cake

Yields 10-16 servings

My mother-in-law Geraldine Vaucresson, affectionately called Mamére by her grandchildren, was a total chocoholic. She loved God, her family, and chocolate. One of her chocolate favorites was Heavenly Hash Cake. Heavenly Hash Easter eggs, have appeared in Louisiana children's baskets for more than 100 years. Mamére was a character who was so full of life, she could have a book of her own. This recipe gives me many warm thoughts of her.

1 cup butter
2 cups sugar
4 eggs, beaten
1½ cups sifted flour
1½ tsps. baking powder
¼ cup cocoa
2 cups chopped pecans
2 tsps. vanilla
3 cups miniature marshmallows

Preheat oven to 350 degrees

With an electric mixer, cream together butter and sugar. Add eggs. Gradually add the dry ingredients and mix well. Mix in pecans and vanilla.

Bake in a greased 13x9-inch pan at 350 degrees for 40 minutes. Remove the cake from the oven and immediately cover with marshmallows. Finish by pouring icing over the cake.

Icing
1 lb. of sifted powdered sugar
¼ cup cocoa
½ cup evaporated milk
¼ cup butter melted

Beat all ingredients together with an electric mixer until smooth, then pour over the cake.

Ooey Gooey Cake

Yields 12 servings

Vance doesn't eat much during the day, but he loves his sweets at night while watching Sports Center. He unwinds after a long day, watching all the highlights, and enjoying something sweet. Ooey gooey cake is one of his favorites. He settles in his recliner with a large glass of milk and a couple of squares of ooey gooey to relax in his happy place.

4 large eggs
1 cup butter, melted
1 15.25-oz. box of yellow cake mix
8 oz. package of cream cheese softened
1 tsp. vanilla extract
3¾ cups of powdered sugar

Preheat oven to 350 degrees.

Mix 2 eggs with butter and cake mix. Spread on the bottom of a greased 9x13 inch baking dish.

Mix the two remaining eggs, cream cheese, vanilla extract, and powdered sugar together until well blended and creamy. Spread cream cheese mixture over cake mix crust and bake at 350 degrees for 35-40 minutes until golden brown. Serve in generous squares.

Fudge

Yields 36 pieces

Every year for Vance's birthday, my mom makes fudge for him. She delivers it in a tin container that she insists he return to her so she can use it again the next year. Not only does Vance look forward to his birthday fudge, but he doesn't share. He loves to eat that fudge late at night, sitting in his recliner watching Sports Center.

4 cups sugar
4 tbsp. cocoa
⅛ tsp. salt
1 cup whole milk
1 cup evaporated milk
2 tbsp. light corn syrup
8 tbsp. butter

Combine sugar, cocoa, and salt. Stir in whole and evaporated milk and corn syrup. Cook over medium heat until sugar dissolves, stirring constantly. Cover and cook for 3 minutes.

Remove cover and do not stir the fudge during the final cooking process. Continue cooking the fudge until the candy thermometer reads 236 degrees. Immediately remove from heat and stir in butter. Cool to lukewarm.

Beat fudge until thick then pour into a greased 9-inch square pan. When cold, cut into 1½ inch squares.

How to Cook Fresh Vaucresson Sausage

Stove—Old School way is in a cast iron skillet (you can use any skillet or frying pan) with a little water, turning periodically. When the water cooks off, keep turning the sausage in the pan, allowing it to brown.

Oven—Place in an oven-safe pan and roast at 350 degrees for about 12 to 15 minutes, turning midway. Poke holes in the sausage to allow the juice to render out.

Grill—Grill over indirect heat and monitor until internal temperature reaches 165 degrees. Turn periodically until casing is seared to your liking. Searing helps give the casing a crisp texture.

You can parboil your sausage before putting it on the grill to cook it internally faster without drying it out. If you place sausage on a direct heat grill, turn frequently to sear to your liking and don't forget to poke holes to allow rendering. This will help sear faster, but may cause a flare up on your grill, so be careful.

Secrets to "Creolizing" a Dish

Having Vaucresson sausage on hand is an easy way to bring out the Creole in any dish. The extra grease and drippings from cooking the sausage should never be discarded. Save that precious flavor in a jar in your refrigerator and use it in place of oil anytime you're cooking seasoning vegetables or when you make a roux.

Where's the salt? Anytime a dish needs salt, I use Creole seasoning instead. In the spice section of Louisiana's grocery

Linda working Jazz Fest.

stores there are shelves and shelves of it to choose from. Do a little experimentation until you find your favorite.

The countless hot sauces of Louisiana also work as a salt substitute. Just make sure to use one that doesn't have too much heat but adds lots of pepper flavor, like Crystal hot sauce.

ACKNOWLEDGEMENTS

My heartfelt gratitude to my husband Vance, and children VJ, Hilary, and Kyce for their endless love and unwavering support. Without their patience, encouragement, and inspiration this project wouldn't have been possible. Thank you to my siblings and friends for their understanding, laughs, and helpful suggestions. A very special thanks to my mother for always being my rock and to my sister Angela for putting up with me and helping me in ways that are unimaginable.

I am most grateful to Poppy Tooker for providing her invaluable mentorship and expertise. Because of Poppy, my dream has become a reality. I am so humbled to have worked with her and am very proud to now, call her a friend.

This project has been a journey of personal growth and development. Thank you to all who have touched my life and made me who I am today.

Julie and Vance with Hoda Kotb and Jenna Bush Hager on the Today *show*

INDEX